Shahram Chubin

Whither Iran?

Reform, Domestic Politics and National Security

Adelphi Paper 342

Oxford University Press, Great Clarendon Street, Oxford OX2 6DP
Oxford   New York
Athens Auckland Bangkok Bombay Calcutta Cape Town
Dar es Salaam Delhi Florence Hong Kong Istanbul Karachi
Kuala Lumpur Madras Madrid Melbourne Mexico City
Nairobi Paris Singapore Taipei Tokyo Toronto
and associated companies in
Berlin Ibadan

Oxford is a trade mark of Oxford University Press

Published in the United States
by Oxford University Press Inc., New York

First published April 2002 by **Oxford University Press** for
The International Institute for Strategic Studies
Arundel House, 13–15 Arundel Street, Temple Place, London WC2R 3DX
www.iiss.org

Director John Chipman
Editor Mats R. Berdal
Assistant Editor John Wheelwright

British Library Cataloguing in Publication Data
Data available

Library of Congress Cataloguing in Publication Data

ISBN 0-19-851667-3
ISSN 0567-932x

Contents

Glossary

AFP	Agence France Presse
BBC	British Broadcasting Corporation
BWC	Biological Weapons Convention
CIA	Central Intelligence Agency
CNN	Cable News Network
CWC	Chemical Weapons Convention
EU	European Union
FBIS NES	Foreign Broadcast Information Service, Near East Service (US government agency)
GCC	Gulf Co-operation Council
IAEA	International Atomic Energy Agency
IRGC	Islamic Revolutionary Guard Corps (or *Pasdaran*)
IRI	Islamic Republic of Iran (name used since 1979)
IRNA	Islamic Republic News Agency
MENA	Middle East News Agency
MKOI	*Mujahiddin-e Khalq* Organisation (Islamic) (Iranian opposition force hosted by Iraq)
MTCR	Missile Technology Control Regime
NATO	North Atlantic Treaty Organisation
NGO	Non-Governmental Organisation
NPT	Non-Proliferation Treaty
NWS	Nuclear-Weapons State(s)
OIC	Organisation for the Islamic Conference
PKK	Kurdistan Workers Party
SAM	Surface-to-Air Missile

SCIRI	Supreme Council for the Islamic Revolution in Iraq (Iraqi opposition force hosted by Iran)
SNSC	Supreme National Security Council
SPA	Saudi Press Agency
TMD	Theatre Missile Defence
UN	United Nations
UNMOVIC	United Nations Monitoring, Verification and Inspection Commission
UNSCOM	United Nations Special Commission
WMD	Weapons of Mass Destruction

Terms

Ayatollah	(literally, 'sign of God') Senior clerical rank in Shia Islam. (Grand Ayatollah is more senior still.)
Basij	Volunteer militia, organised as a form of territorial guard, subordinate to the IRGC
fatwa	Religious edict issued by senior clerics which, in theory, can only be rescinded by them
Hezbollah	(literally, 'party of God') Name adopted by various paramilitary groups that grew out of the 1979 Revolution and answer to various Iranian power centres or individuals. The Lebanese Hezbollah is both a Shi'i political party and a resistance organisation, and has been inspired and funded by Iran
Hojjatoleslam	(literally, 'proof of Islam') Shi'i clerical rank immediately below Ayatollah; can be acquired after some 15–20 years of study

Dramatis Personae

FALLAHIAN, Ali   Member of the Assembly of Experts, former Minister of Information (Intelligence and Security) 1989–97; Vice Minister 1984–89. Considered a hard-liner.

JANNATI, Ahmad (Ayatollah)   Secretary of the Council of Guardians; member of the Assembly of Experts since 1980. Member of Expediency Council. A hard-liner.

KHAMENE'I, Sayyed Ali (Ayatollah)   Supreme Leader of the Revolution (*rahbar*) from June 1989; Jurisprudent Ruler of the IRI; Commander-in-Chief of Armed Forces; president of IRI from 1981–89; Commander of the IRGC; member of the Supreme Defence Council. Moderate conservative?

KHARRAZI, Kamal   Foreign Minister since 1997; ambassador to the UN from 1989–97; member of the Supreme Council for Defence from 1980–89 (formed for coordination and planning during the Iran–Iraq war). A reformist.

KHATAMI, Mohammad (Hojjatoleslam)   President since 1997; Director of the National Library from 1992–97; former minister of Culture and Islamic Guidance in the cabinets of President Rafsanjani and Prime Minister Mirhossein Mousavi, from 1981–92. Moderate reformist.

MOHAJERANI, Ataollah   Head of the Center for Dialogue of Civilisations; former minister of Culture and Islamic Guidance from 1997–2000 (forced to resign); Vice President between 1989–97. A reformist.

MOHTASHEMIPOUR, Ali Akbar Member of the 6th *Majlis* for Tehran and member of the 3rd *Majlis* from 1988–92; minister of interior from 1985–9; ambassador to Syria from 1981–85. A key supporter of Hezbollah in 1980. An Islamic leftist, now a reformist in domestic politics, who is one of the few who continues to support the violent export of the revolution.

MONTAZERI, Hossein Ali (Grand Ayatollah) (source of emulation, highest level of Shi'ite theological scholarship) Under house arrest; designated successor to Ayatollah Khomeini from 1985–89, dismissed from leadership 1989. Opposed to the concept of a rahbar, and hence a reformist on this issue.

NOURI, Abdollah Hosseinabadi Prominent reformer jailed by the Special Clerical Court in December 1999 for advocating reforms considered dangerous by the conservatives. Vice President from 1997–99; editor of the reformist newspaper *Khordad*; member of Expediency Council; President Rafsanjani's appointee as chairman of the Supreme National Security Council; representative of Ayatollah Khomein'i to the IRGC; Interior Minister.

RAFSANJANI, Akbar Hashemi Bahramani (Ayatollah) Chairman of the Expediency Council since 1997; member of Assembly of Experts; Occasional Friday Preacher of Tehran; President of the Islamic Republic from 1989–97; Chairman of Supreme National Security Council 1989–97; acting Commander-in-Chief of the Armed Forces from 1987–88; Speaker of the *Majlis*, from 1981–89. A leading figure both formally and informally. Considered a liberal when president, he has moved increasingly towards the conservatives (many think as a result of personal pique at reformists' criticisms).

RAHIM-SAFAVI, Yahya Commander-in-Chief of the IRGC from 1997, Deputy Commander in the period 1990–97. Considered a hardliner.

REZA'I, Mohsen Secretary of the Expediency Council since 1997; Founding Member of the IRGC, Commander-in-Chief of the IRGC from 1980–97. A leading hardliner.

ROWHANI (Rouhani), Hasan (Hojjatoleslam) Member of the Expediency Council; member of Assembly of Experts; representative of Ayatollah Khamene'i and Secretary-General of the Supreme Council of National Security; Deputy Speaker of the *Majlis* from 1992–2000. His political orientation is difficult to identify.

SHAHBAZI, Ali Supreme Commander of the Armed Forces (i.e. the regular military, as distinct from the IRGC) from 1998. Moderate reformist?

SHAMKHANI, Ali Minister of Defence since 1997; Commander of IRGC naval forces from 1989–97, and IRGC ground forces in 1985–88. A traditionalist rightist hard-liner on security, who argued for expanding the war with Iraq to its supporters, Kuwait and Saudi Arabia.

VELAYATI, Ali-Akbar Advisor to the Supreme Leader on Foreign Affairs since 1997; member of the Expediency Council; ex-officio member of the Supreme Council of National Security; Minister of Foreign Affairs from 1981–97. Now considered a hard-liner.

YAZDI, Mohammad (Ayatollah) Member of the Assembly of Experts; member of the Council of Guardians; member of the Expediency Council; occasional Friday Preacher; Head of Judiciary from 1989–99. A strict conservative.

Introduction

Iran, as an Islamic republic, has been a major factor for instability for the past two decades. The country is situated in a strategically important and volatile area, and its policies have a significant impact on regional security in the Persian Gulf, the Caucasus and the wider Middle East and South Asia. Under domestic pressure, Iran has been struggling to redefine itself: to give new and relevant meaning to the concept of an 'Islamic republic'; to reconcile Islamic rule with the demand for democracy; to find a balance between the country's national culture and its Islamic identity; and to reconcile the need to play a significant international role so as to further Iran's own interests with the requirements of solidarity with other states, Muslim or 'oppressed'. The outcome of Iran's power struggle will define its international role and have an important impact on its strategy. How Iran defines and chooses to pursue its interests, what resources it dedicates to this, and indeed, how it views the world, will influence the security of the region. Moreover, since its past behaviour has been disruptive, notably its use of terrorism and development of weapons of mass destruction, a change in Iran's policies has potentially wider significance.

In the past five years, with generational change and demographic pressures reflected in economic and social tensions, politics in Iran have been transformed into something resembling an open, quasi-democratic system. Though profound, and many would agree 'irreversible',[1] this transformation has led to a power struggle that is ambiguous and whose course is uncertain. Its impact on foreign and security policy, potentially very significant, is still unclear.

This Paper seeks to assess the impact that the reformist movement has had on Iran's foreign relations and national security, and to ask to what extent the perceptions and priorities of the 'reformers' differ from those of the 'conservatives' (to be defined) and to what extent the reformers are, or will be, in a position to deliver on them. In brief, the focus is on the impact of domestic change on Iran's national security policy.

The paper is divided into five chapters and a conclusion. The first chapter looks at the achievements of the reformists in foreign policy so far, compares the respective world views of the two tendencies, and discusses the relationship between domestic politics and foreign policy and the areas of similarity or convergence between the two groups. Chapter 2 contains a discussion of defence doctrine, threat perceptions and strategic approach and a particular example of its employment. Chapter 3 assesses missiles in Iran's strategy and looks at this strategy's impact on Israel. Chapter 4 examines Iran's nuclear ambitions and the constraints affecting them. Chapter 5 looks at Iran's use of terrorism and its policy on the issue of Palestine. In each case, policy is discussed in light of the actual or potential impact of the reformists in these areas. To avoid replicating existing literature, the emphasis will be on whatever detectable and significant differences affecting national security there are, or might be, between the two groups contending for power in Iran, and the broader implications of these differences for security.

The Conclusion looks to the future and considers how things might change and what policies the Western states might reasonably adopt in the light of a continuing, prolonged and ambiguous struggle for power in Iran.

My thesis is that Iran is undergoing significant political change that has implications for the definition and pursuit of national security. A visible part of this seismic change in the political and social landscape is reflected in the 'reformist' movement. This movement – more a 'tendency' than a coherent or unified party – reflects many currents of thought and is focused primarily on domestic issues. Hence it does not articulate a unified foreign or national-security policy in opposition to that of its conservative, or hard-line, opponents. Nonetheless, the reformist tendency is animated by a different view of the world, and in time this could translate into a national-security policy that is less assertive, defiant and centred on force.

I do *not* argue that the 'reformists' have a different or alternative set of national-security policies, nor that a debate has been joined with the conservatives on the most contentious issues of policy, notably relating to the interwoven subjects of WMD, terrorism and the Middle East. Rather, I show in the first part of the paper that the net effect of the reformists so far has been to change foreign policy in two difficult and controversial areas (*vis-à-vis* the Salman Rushdie issue, and relations with Saudi Arabia). I also seek to show that while the two 'camps' agree on certain fundamental principles (independence, equality, respect and the need for enhanced status and a greater role for Iran), they may not agree in their detail or application. For example, whereas Ayatollah Khamene'i, the Supreme Leader, sees globalisation as a cultural threat and prefers isolation, President Khatami denies that this is a viable policy and seeks engagement and dialogue as an opportunity. Differences on foreign policy – which Khatami effectively controls (with the exception of relations with the US and Israel) – are significant. Such differences potentially play out in the harder areas of national security as well.

Given the shrouded nature of decision-making on security matters and the fact that issues like terrorism, and whether or not to seek nuclear weapons, do not lend themselves to public or official discussion, it is difficult to identify either a formal defence doctrine or an official debate on the pros and cons of nuclear weapons. I have sought to identify Iran's defence doctrine by analysing its threat perceptions. Missiles and their envisaged likely uses and doctrine are somewhat easier, because, unlike nuclear weapons, they are not banned by treaty, and statements have been made and postures adopted.

Despite this caveat, I have focused on the three related issues of terrorism, missiles and nuclear weapons because of their intrinsic importance to both Iran and the West. I seek to show that the rationale for missile acquisition and potential use does not appear to be disputed, so this issue is unlikely to be affected by any change in power that favoured the reformists, or by any extension of their control over the national-security apparatus. Nuclear weapons are banned, and Iran formally denies a wish to acquire any. The rationale for going toward a nuclear *option* may be convincing, but the constraints on moving in this direction and the difficulties of converting such an option into either political leverage or a real weapons capability are both formidable. This issue, by its nature, cannot be debated officially, but there is discussion in the public sphere. As the costs of seeking an undetected nuclear weapons option increase, as the domestic environment makes the continuation of secret programmes more difficult, and as Iran engages with the world more normally, the incentives for going down this path will decline.

By contrast, Iranian use of terrorism has changed considerably. Although the question has not been openly debated, there now appears to be a consensus that reflexive reliance on terrorism is, in general, both immoral and counterproductive. (As we shall see, in the one area in which terrorism is still used – Palestine – it is still seen as legally and morally justified.) There are several reasons for this, including a domestic one: the total discrediting of terrorism as an instrument of policy after its use to settle domestic political agendas. The residual use of terrorism in the service of the Palestinian cause depends on the course of Iran's Middle East policy. Here too, while there has been no official debate, there has been more public discussion; most Iranians feel solidarity with the Palestinians, but the discussion is only just beginning to address what this might involve in terms of the level, kind and cost of support.

Different world views, and the consequences of greater Iranian involvement in international relations, will make a reformist Iran less likely to pursue a nuclear option, or to encourage settlement of the Palestinians' legitimate aims by military means. I argue that this will come about not because the reformists are likely to gain control of national-security institutions very soon, nor because they have a clear and competing concept of national security, but because their different world view will create different priorities and a different view of security. In addition, they are encouraging and inculcating a tradition of sceptical debate and questioning of issues; this will in time extend even to the most sensitive areas of national security. A pluralist, reformist Iran may not be a liberal democracy, but it will be more transparent and less ideologically motivated. Even as a nationalist state pursuing an independent agenda, it will be a more reassuring to live with than its ideological, revolutionary predecessor.

Chapter 1

Reform and Foreign Policy

Mohammad Khatami ran for President in 1997 on a platform of change that focused mainly on domestic issues, but its foreign-policy component – normalisation with Iran's neighbours and Europe – was popular with the electorate. Once elected, Khatami changed policy in these two areas, which had been politically contentious. This success was nonetheless notable because, in reversing policy toward the GCC and the EU, Khatami had to contravene two express injunctions of Ayatollah Khomeini, whose will and testament (in the case of relations with Saudi Arabia) and *fatwa* (in the case of Salman Rushdie) had been major obstacles to change. Khatami's success in surmounting these obstacles suggests flexibility and pragmatism on the part of the regime, where its interests are directly concerned. The implication of this is that given a perception of need, nothing stands in the way of similar pragmatism motivating policy on the Middle East issue.

Domestic Politics and Foreign Policy

Foreign and domestic policies are tightly linked in revolutionary (and hence highly ideological) states. Iran has been ideological but not suicidal, tempering ideology with pragmatism when regime security was at stake, as in the 1986 'Irangate' episode, among others. After the end of the war with Iraq in 1988, Iran emphasised 'reconstruction' under President Rafsanjani (1988–1997) and now 'development' under President Khatami (1997 to date).[1] Throughout the Rafsanjani period, foreign policy was an extension of factional politics, which resulted in incoherence, obstructionism and multiple centres of decision-making.[2]

This has continued under Khatami, though with the difference that Khatami has greater popular, domestic legitimacy and greater acceptance abroad. Ideology continues to have an influence (former President Rafsanjani equates Iran's militant activism abroad as part of its revolutionary, Islamic identity, and sees its relinquishment as a decision to become merely an 'ordinary' state[3]) and, as I shall show, Khatami remains hamstrung by the remnants of an ideological approach to foreign and security policy, especially in respect to relations with the US.[4]

Ideology has distorted reality and blinkered its adherents, who have used it as an instrument of political competition to undermine or inhibit their opponents. What is new in the Khatami period is the clear primacy and urgency of domestic issues, and the need to address these. Foreign-policy activism is no longer seen as a substitute for meeting the growing domestic crisis; rather, foreign policy is now seen as a possible way to reduce pressure on the regime, by ending isolation and increasing its access to resources, investment, etc. Foreign policy, though it might *contribute* to domestic performance, can no longer replace it.

Domestic political issues have the highest priority in contemporary Iran, in the absence of urgent or overriding (external) security issues. The accumulation of grave domestic problems, including unemployment, inflation, economic mismanagement, corruption and restrictive social policies, have brought the Islamic republic to the verge of breakdown. Against this backdrop of persistent decline and incipient crisis, there is an intensified struggle for power, which ultimately reflects different visions of how Iran ought to be defined and develop. Differences over how to respond to generational, demographic, political, economic and social pressures are often depicted as ideological. In fact they mask the more mundane and base defence of material vested interests and power by conservatives resisting reform for fear of losing their control of economic institutions (the parastatal foundations) and the security organisations.

The stark reality is that on the eve of Khatami's election as president in 1997 Islamic Iran had reached a political and economic dead-end. The younger generation (some 65% of the population is under thirty), the children of the revolution, had largely become alienated by the incompetence, repression, corruption and rhetoric of the leadership. There were various reasons for this, including strict social controls, but a primary ingredient was the mismanagement of the country's economic resources that is now resulting in a potentially wealthy nation sliding into poverty and decline. Persistent large-scale unemployment and resultant emigration of the educated classes (some 200,000 a year were leaving before 1997) were testimony to this; yet, despite talk of the dangers of 'losing the nation's youth', little had been done about it. The conservatives hoped that Khatami's election would have a calming effect, and that his foreign policy of normalisation with Iran's neighbours and Europe would yield domestic political dividends. In reality, Iran's economic prospects depend on major structural reforms, including widespread privatisation of the large, profitable and unaccountable parastatal foundations run by Ayatollah Sayyed Ali Khamene'i, the Supreme Leader, and his political allies: i.e., those with vested interests. In the absence of this, and of the systematic and dependable application of the rule of law, Iran is unlikely to stimulate and liberate the private investment it needs.[5] The key point is that, even if Khatami showed leadership qualities and expertise in the economic area, it is doubtful whether he would be able, or be permitted, to carry out the necessary reforms. Khatami's role as lightning-rod for the regime's critics is thus a thankless one. The Khatami phenomenon both reflects and encourages a growing, questioning, civil society that demands the right to be included in and to influence decision-making, prompted by a new sense of scepticism about the received wisdom that the regime's religious and political authorities transmit. The hardliners accept the need for some accommodation of this phenomenon without accepting the need for the structural reforms that are necessary if it is to be effective.

While Khatami both reflects and reinforces the forces calling for change, his allies are not homogeneous or united on any particular set of policies. Similarly, the conservative elements are a mixed bag, some more conservative than the Supreme Leader, some less. Khatami himself has characterised the political competition between the two factions thus: 'At any rate one political tendency firmly believes in the prevalence of logic and the rule of law, while there might be another tendency that believes it is entitled to go beyond the law'.[6]

The political competition between reformist and conservative is deceptive and complex.[7] Each tendency encompasses a wide spectrum, and the differences between the two groupings are not always as wide as portrayed. While conservatives might encompass the old merchants (bazaar), the reformists might gain the support of the more free-market 'new' bazaar. Not all reformists are proponents of a free market, and many are 'old left' and radical on foreign policy. The conservatives are characterised by those supporting clerical control of power and patronage, but many clerics do *not* support such a role, and are behind the reformists, notably Ayatollah Montazeri.[8]

Because of the overlap between the two 'factions' on certain issues, the political competition in contemporary Iran is not polarised, but it has intensified since 1997. Ostensibly about the details and modalities of government within an Islamic republic – how to define and operationalise 'Islamic democracy'; the kind of leadership (elected or appointed?); the role of popular sovereignty and the rule of law; the place of the clerics (in the mosque or in government?); and accountability of government and freedom of expression – these differences go to the very heart of the definition of, and control of, Iranian politics. The urgency to meet Iran's crises that is felt by the political establishment, and has given rise to the phenomenon represented by President Khatami, has granted him the leeway for some reform, but the conservative beneficiaries of the current order are not reassured that their interests will be untouched by those same reforms.

At the core of President Khatami's reforms is his tolerance and encouragement of debate and criticism, and his enthusiastic support for popular sovereignty. This has brought him and his supporters victory in four elections in four years – two presidential (1997, 2001), one parliamentary (2000) and one in local councils (1999), each time with a majority of some 70%. These electoral successes, in turn, have empowered the people to express themselves, and to hold their leaders accountable for their acts. The conservatives fear that authority will pass from the divine to the popular, and that their alleged basis for power (always obscure) will be held up to the light and be found wanting, as religious legitimacy is replaced by *performance* legitimacy. For them, therefore, the entire reform project is two-edged: it promises to ameliorate the profound crisis facing the country and regime, and is therefore necessary, but it also threatens their grip on (indeed their very claim to) power.

For the conservatives three considerations are paramount. First, can the regime in fact be reformed, or will it disintegrate in the process? The 'Gorbachev analogy' is often invoked in Iranian politics; reflecting this ambivalence, the Supreme Leader, Khamene'i, has depicted the process of reform as an elaborate American plot, but noted that in Iran, in contrast to the Soviet Union, the people support the system.[9] Second, there is the question of the nature of the reforms and who benefits from them. A change *in* the regime might become a change *of* regime. This most obviously affects the role of the Supreme Leader, whose prerogatives include control of the security forces and media, and vast patronage networks and connections with shadowy groups of vigilantes, who, in the last analysis, guarantee his position.[10] Erosion of control over the formal instruments of power could see a total transformation of the system; this will be resisted, if necessary, by reliance on the informal instruments of repression.

Related to this is the question of relative gain: who (that is, which faction) benefits from reform? Reforms intended to bolster the system might strengthen the hand of one faction at the expense of the other; this accounts for the conservatives' persistent tendency to try to sabotage Khatami's foreign policies, notwithstanding an apparent consensus on the need for foreign-policy adjustment. The key point here is that, while change in foreign policy is less contentious (in part because less is at stake in terms of domestic political control and power), it is still seen as having possible domestic repercussions on the standing of the respective factions. Conservatives have consistently tried to depict reformers as US agents, disturbances as foreign plots, and differences as providing fertile ground for foreign exploitation.[11]

Foreign policy and national security, far from being depoliticised under Khamene'i, remain an extension of factional politics. This is most evident in cases such as Tehran's autumn 1998 confrontation with the Taliban regime in Kabul over the murder of Iranian diplomats and treatment of Shia Afghans. Conservatives sought to intensify the crisis, to depict the reformists as weak and to use the resultant atmosphere to increase domestic repression.[12] Three years later, in another crisis over Afghanistan, the conservatives did everything to ensure that Iran did not work closely with the US, lest the reformers should benefit. Such factionalism weakens foreign policy, and reformers have noted how politicisation has inhibited serious, dispassionate discussion of issues, notably ties with the US.[13]

For the conservatives, the issue is how to use foreign policy to strengthen the regime, without giving the reformists any chance to take the credit for its successes. For the reformists, the problem is how to use foreign policy to meet Iran's growing needs – including improving its international standing and increasing its influence and voice – and to use the legitimacy gained thereby to push for further changes *domestically.*

Given the domestic power struggle, the major focus in Iran has been on the impact foreign and security policies have on domestic politics and the relative standing of the factions. The prime concern here is the degree to which domestic politics has affected national security policy, or has the potential to do so.

The proposition that a more tolerant regime in Iran will pursue more moderate goals externally, and that a more democratically legitimate regime will be easier to deal with, seems intuitively sound. Whether it applies to Iran remains unclear. Analysts have made the case that a popular president has a stronger foreign hand to play,[14] and Khatami's own Ministers have made the same point.[15] Khatami himself has argued that foreign policy must reflect a strong system: 'This means [the necessity for] close ties between the system and the people'.[16] Underlining the relationship between internal and external factors, he noted that: 'We all know that the fabricated crises of recent years have not had a suitable effect on our internal relations or international standing'.[17]

Foreign powers have assumed that the domestic transformation heralds a new chapter in Iran's foreign relationships, to which they should respond. They have also argued the necessity for supporting Khatami through engagement in order to buttress him in the domestic power struggle. In 1999 France's Foreign Minister Hubert Vedrine defended Khatami's visit to Paris in precisely these terms.[18] At about the same time, the US tried to assess how far the change in the Presidency foreshadowed change in policy by addressing a secret note directly to Khatami, asking for assistance in solving a terrorism case in which Iran was allegedly involved. (The response was not encouraging.[19]) Israel, too, has been torn between a natural scepticism that Khatami represents a real departure from policies that threaten Israel's security and the possibility that he reflects real change in a society that is undergoing a transformation, and so represents a chance to establish a new relationship.[20]

A consensus foreign view appears to be that, even if Khatami's powers are curtailed, he has had *some* successes in foreign policy (notably in the Persian Gulf and with the EU), and he remains 'a force for stability in a volatile region in spite of his limited powers'. The conclusion is that western powers ought to encourage him and make clear that 'continued international backing depends on democratic progress at home as well as Iran's behaviour in the region. They must also warn against Iranian support for radical groups in the Middle East and monitor closely allegations of Iranian attempts to acquire weapons of mass destruction.'[21] However, efforts to link good relations with Iran to policy changes can be depicted by conservatives as attempts to dictate to Iran and dilute its independence, and thus lay reformists open to the charge of being 'foreign agents'. Similarly, attempts to restore dialogue or normalise relations with states like Israel remain vulnerable to acts of sabotage by hard-liners opposed to any opening up.[22]

Khatami's and Khamene'i's World Views: Contrasts and Similarities

Khatami's view of the world is very different from that of the Supreme Leader, Khamene'i. The principal difference between the two factions is the importance they attach to Islam as opposed to Iranian nationalism. The difference is significant because, while both want Iran to play a leading international role, they differ on what sort of role Iran should play, in whose interest the policy should function, and ultimately also on the price worth paying for this role.

Khamene'i's view is very much a relic of the early revolutionary era; the world is a 'jungle ... every thing we do is a battle. Life is a battlefield'. Iran should cultivate 'loneliness' and retain a closed system. Embattlement is inevitable and ennobling.[23] In this view, threats are multidimensional and stem from cultural contact and the contamination that accompanies globalisation:

> *Audio and visual waves, which are worse than warplanes, are being used to disseminate a rogue culture aimed at reasserting the domination of the enemies of Islam, paving the way for the imposition of unethical values and Western-ised ideas to captivate and humiliate Muslims.*[24]
>
> *The United States seeks to dictate and control other states; therefore Iran should realise its unique destiny by confronting the arrogant unipolar power, at whatever price, welcoming the cost as the price to be paid for true independence.*[25]

Khamene'i sees Iran as leading the world of Islam in resisting military and cultural pressures from the US to establish relations – relations that would then compromise the youth of the country, the nation's spiritual values and its political independence. He therefore resists any form of dialogue with the United States as being inherently one-sided. 'They want to have authority. They want to make decisions. That is what globalisation means.'[26] Related to this view is the need for vigilance against sinister plots and infiltration, suggesting constant mobilisation of the faithful. Khamene'i had often contrasted this loyal constituency with the 'Westoxicated' elements (supporting the reformists). Khamene'i sees Iran as the only power able and willing to stand up for principle (spiritual values) and to confront the multi-dimensional threat represented by the United States. He refers to Iran's independence and 'sovereignty over its own destiny [as being] on the basis of Islam and the holy Koran'.[27]

Khatami, too, perceives external threats and pressures, but he does not see remaining isolated as either a practical solution or especially ennobling; 'We cannot close the doors completely', and his solution is to 'immunize people'.[28] He has elaborated this over time:

> *No country can afford to form its cultural, political, economic and social policies without taking world events into account. And it is simply not possible in today's world. [Despite differences in interest and power, there is a degree of interdependence and] this means that in all relations and dealings a balance can be struck, which takes into account the position of both parties.*

Following on he argues that democratisation, in which power flows from the people, will 'bring us a true sense of identity and pride', with the 'state becoming the representative of the nation and defender of national interests'.[29]

Khatami sees no inevitable or necessary conflict between Iran and its neighbours or major powers. He sees Iran's past policies as unnecessarily confrontational and is concerned about the costs of those policies. Above all, he emphasises the domestic dimension of power, including the 'cultural and historical identity of the Iranian nation' as 'two solid pillars' of Iran's foreign policy: 'Making enemies is not a skill; real skill lies in the ability to neutralise enemies, convert animosities to human interactions and scale down hostilities ... And, this is not incompatible with our principles'.[30] He is aware also of the relationship between his aim of empowering the people through democracy and foreign policy – that is, of the inter-related domestic and foreign dimensions of the continuing political rivalry in Iran: 'Being mighty does not mean fighting the world at any cost, and debate does not mean abandoning the principles and values of society and revolution'.[31]

Unlike Khamene'i, Khatami does not need to stir up emotions or hatred for political support. For Khamene'i, Iran represents a model of revolutionary Islam: militant, defiant and activist. For Khatami, Iran represents a model for Islamic *democracy*:

> *Religious rule of the people is our model for the world. And any attempt which stands against this movement will be an act of treachery against the interests of the nation. [This implies defence of the] oppressed and deprived throughout the world, by virtue of independence, freedom and magnanimity, and by relying on your interests.*[32]

Khatami is suggesting here that Iran's greatest contribution to the deprived is by improving its own model of Islamic democracy and the values it represents, and, by implication, not by indiscriminate interventions abroad.

In the election campaign for a second term (in which foreign policy barely figured), Khatami suggested there were three approaches to foreign policy:

> *One is to give in. That is to say, we would give in and surrender in the face of world mastery, the international system and the wishes of the powerful ...*
>
> *The other is absolute idealism, whereby we would not see the realities at all and we would make ourselves happy with a series of slogans – which could not even be realised without real resources.*
>
> *The third approach, which I think desirable, is – while relying on ideals and the correct direction – to deal with the world with realism.*[33]

Unlike Khamene'i, Khatami emphasises Iranian nationalism, pre-Islamic history and culture and the need to concentrate on Iran's national interests. 'An Islamic society can take pride in its identity and in its past.'[34] He insists that Iran's foreign policy is based on the principles and values of national interest, and in his speeches in the countryside has been known to say 'first comes Iran, then Islam'.[35]

There is considerable evidence that the new generation of Iranians – the majority – is most responsive to the appeals of nationalism. Pride in being Iranian is one of the values that transcends other differences in Iran, and it is a more inclusive conception of citizenship than the religious. The image of an Iran

more engaged in international affairs, emphasising popular sovereignty as well as Islam, and focusing on Iran's national interest
with a sense of realism about power realities and costs, creates a
very different picture from the one conveyed by mindless activism,
insensitive to costs and open-ended in its commitments to defy and
fight 'threats', whether cultural, moral or political. Khatami's foreign policy is based on dialogue without rhetoric, and on an
attempt to build trust and confidence through measures that Iran
and its neighbours can jointly support to their mutual benefit.

These differences should not be overstated. Iranians share a
view about Iran's history, and an ambition for its future role, that
transcends political orientation. They share a sense of pride in
being Iranian, but at the same time see their country as having
been subjected to imperialist designs that left it manipulated,
plundered, exploited, bereft of dignity and even identity. In this
view, Iran's problems started with foreign influence: the source of
all its woes. This pervasive sense of victimisation has developed
into an all-purpose alibi and excuse for failures, current and past.
While inhibiting a sense of responsibility and honest self-appraisal,
it has imbued Iranians with a sense of the paramount need for
independence and the right to pursue their own path.[36] This has left
Iran with an 'anti-imperialist sensibility'.[37]

Another goal shared by nationalists (monarchical or republi-
can, secular or religious) is that Iran ought to play an important
role internationally. It should 'punch above its weight'; it should be
a regional power and global player. Khamene'i, in his quest to
keep the country mobilised and vigilant has expressed this, noting
that 'today you are a nation with an important opinion to express',
and that no international issue can be resolved without Iran's
agreement. Khatami's approach is more reflective, putting an emphasis on reciprocity:

> *We have to know who we are. We are Iranian and Muslim.*
> *We are a civilized people. We have an exceptional position in*
> *the region and the world. The world needs us. The world*
> *needs us for what we have. We have to know about their*
> *needs when establishing relations with them.*[38]

Khatami and Khamene'i's views of the world influence Iran's

policies; Khatami has (largely) taken control of foreign affairs, but defence remains an area controlled by Khamene'i. The result is incongruous and inconsistent, in that the two approaches – confidence-building and co-operative security, on the one hand, and self-reliance and emphasis on military security, on the other – are not synchronised.

Two Areas of Concrete Achievement: The EU and the Gulf

Khatami ran for President in 1997 on a platform emphasising 'tension-reduction' and détente with Iran's immediate neighbours. Iran was at the time virtually isolated from the Arab states in the Persian Gulf, while relations with the European Union (EU) were in crisis following a German court ruling implicating Iranian government officials in terrorism abroad. Iranians were tired of incessant crises, ashamed of the resultant image and of Iran's marginalisation in international affairs. Khatami's opponents did not challenge him.[39] Khatami's determination to mend fences with the Gulf Co-operation Council (GCC) did not originate with him; his predecessor Rafsanjani had tried it with little success, in part due to domestic differences. Khatami, however, now had an impressive mandate for it. He also came with an unchequered past.

The Gulf

How bad relations were can be judged from a GCC communiqué dating from before Khatami's term, which referred to Iran's interference in Bahrain, to a 'policy of fait accompli by force' over islands disputed with the United Arab Emirates (UAE), and to Iran's 'feverish' acquisition of arms beyond its defence needs.[40] Khatami had every interest in defusing the suspicion and mistrust that this reflected through a more active and cooperative foreign policy of dialogue and confidence-building; this implied 'refraining from any behaviour or activity that could cause tension'.[41]

Khatami's implicit recognition of Iran's responsibility for the tension across the Gulf and his warm manner, combined with a policy of dialogue and his obvious domestic popularity, made him an easier interlocutor for the Gulf states. So too did his preference for national interest over some ever-expansive duty of Islamic leadership that automatically pitched Iran into rivalry with Saudi Arabia.[42] As a result of a change in atmosphere and rhetoric in Tehran the GCC states turned out in force for the Organisation for the Islamic Conference (OIC) summit held under Iran's presidency in November 1997 in Tehran.

In substance, apart from warm words that helped to change the atmosphere, Khatami's policy in the Persian Gulf was not too different from Rafsanjani's. The one exception was that Iran no longer actively assisted in subverting the Gulf states. In other areas – military expenditures, the development of Iran's missile programme, Iran's occupation of disputed islands, and opposition to the US presence – policy remained the same. The Iranian Naval Commander gave expression to both aspects of Khatami's policy:

The naval forces of the army and IRGC [Revolutionary Guards] are prepared to cooperate with forces of other Persian Gulf states to bring sustainable security, peace and stability to the region ...Warmongering, creating tensions and ravaging the economic resource of the regional states are among [the] consequences of the foreign powers' illegitimate presence in the region, specially that of the USA.[43]

Khatami told Iran's military commanders: 'We not only do not need [a] foreign presence to establish security in the region but consider them as the root cause of disputes and confrontations'.[44] The Supreme Leader echoed this: 'The presence of foreign forces created tension and unrest, and Iran sought regional security assured by regional states'.[45]

Khatami's diplomacy consisted of frequent exchanges of messages and visits by himself, Defence Minister Ali Shamkhani and Foreign Minister Kamal Kharrazi (notably to Saudi Arabia, but to most of the smaller states as well).[46] In addition Iran invited the other states of the Gulf to exchange naval visits and military observers, to pursue high level military exchanges, and generally to seek to defuse suspicions about each other. It also sought to reassure the local states about its missile programme (offering, hyperbolically, to put its missiles at the disposal of Saudi Arabia).[47]

Khatami's policy in the Gulf has been to consolidate a system of regional security through bilateral confidence-building measures that might, eventually, lead to an institutionalised regional security arrangement and make the presence of US forces superfluous. So far there have been no takers. However, in early 2001 Iran concluded a 'security agreement' with Saudi Arabia dealing with cooperation in fighting terrorism, drug smuggling and the like. (This is more significant as an indicator of improved relations than as a sign of similar views about security.) Iran hopes to follow this up with similar agreements with other states.

On the politically sensitive issue of the islands disputed with the UAE, Iran has stuck to its earlier position: bilateral talks, not international arbitration or multilateral diplomacy. Despite an improvement in the atmosphere, there has been no substantive progress on this issue.

On the key issue of the United States' military presence in the region, which includes the hosting of forces by some of the GCC states and a regional base structure, Iran and the GCC states also differed. Khatami adhered to the Iranian position that the US presence, built on the 'false' allegation that it was aimed at countering regional threats, was itself a destabilising factor in the region, while the GCC states saw it as essential for a regional balance, whether aimed at Iraq or Iran. However, Tehran has now resorted to a softer, subtler approach to resolving its differences with the GCC over the US presence.

Iran's fence-mending was logical. Whatever the differences, Iran did not want a repetition of the polarisation between Iran and the Arab states (in the Gulf) that had accompanied the Iran–Iraq war, and near-isolation in the Middle East could not be a base for an increase in Iranian influence. Hence the two sides had reasons to play down their differences. How long this can continue will depend on the urgency of the issues that are being avoided. The question of theatre missile defences in the Persian Gulf, which has been broached by the US, will complicate this diplomacy, which depends on minimising controversy.

Khatami has been at pains to show his domestic opponents that his 'détente' policies do not indicate a willingness to compromise the national interest.[48] Notwithstanding the apparent consensus on the need for Iran to break out of its isolation and rebuild ties with the GCC states, and despite Khatami's apparent success in doing this without sacrificing national interests, his Gulf policies have been subject to obstructionism and sabotage. His initial plans to visit Riyadh were postponed after the Revolutionary Guards timed exercises to embarrass him. And the security agreement was delayed for months because of internal differences among the leadership in Iran.[49]

Europe

Another Khatami success has been improving ties with the EU. Iran had long sought, with some success, to prevent a united front between Europe and the United States. The European states were keen to maintain a 'critical dialogue' with Tehran, a channel that would clarify differences and mutual concerns and act as an incentive for restraint on Iran. Iran's continuing involvement in terrorism and the *fatwa* announced by Ayatollah Khomeini against Salman Rushdie, however, set limits to this policy. Even worse, on 10 April 1997 a German court found the Iranian government directly responsible for planning and carrying out the assassination of opposition elements in Berlin (the Mykonos case), handing out indictments against named officials, including the Information (i.e. Intelligence) minister, Ali Fallahian.

Khatami thus took office at a time when EU ambassadors had been recalled 'for consultations'. Despite a popular mandate for 'normalisation', his domestic opponents remained ambivalent. The Supreme Leader, true to form, referred to European impudence, and to the long queue of states seeking to sell goods to Iran. In his view, Iran 'ha[d] no need of Europe'.[50]

Khatami first replaced Fallahian as minister. Thereafter, his more gentle diplomacy of cultural engagement with the West, expressed at the OIC conference in November and again in his CNN interview of January 1998, thawed relations. Within a year the tone of his administration had led to the assessment in the EU that Khatami represented genuine reform, and that he needed support from external powers to anchor and deepen these reforms.

A key obstacle to normalisation with Europe remained the *fatwa* issued by Ayatollah Khomeini against Salman Rushdie. Iran had long argued that *fatwas* could only be rescinded by the issuer. Whatever the merits of such an argument, in September 1998 the Khatami government's willingness to disassociate itself from the *fatwa* and its implementation was accepted as satisfactory and sufficient by the British government. Ambassadors were exchanged in May 1999. Other EU states followed suit.

Subsequent successful visits by Khatami to Italy (March 1999), France (October 1999) and Germany (July 2000) strengthened what was now called 'constructive engagement'. Khatami's aim was to break out of his country's largely self-imposed isolation and to take the case of a now-reforming Iran abroad, above all to international public opinion. There were practical considerations as well: to play on European commercial rivalries, to accentuate the differences between European and American approaches to Iran, and to seek foreign investments and credits. The Iranian leadership recognised that funds would only follow security, and that security was dependent, above all, on the 'rule of law' that must first be established within Iran. Khatami thus sought for Iran a breathing spell, and a more sympathetic public, rather than immediate leaps in investment.

But Khatami's policies were not uncontested. The 15th Khordad Foundation (a quasi-autonomous and financially unaccountable parastatal organ), had put a bounty on Rushdie's murder and insisted on the continuing validity of the *fatwa* and the reward. In February 2001 the IRGC issued a statement that the *fatwa* against Rushdie remained valid and enforceable.[51] Khatami in his second election campaign insisted 'we should consider the question of Salman Rushdie as finished', underlining at the same time Iran's opposition to all types of terrorism.[52] Each of Khatami's foreign visits has elicited criticism or worse from his domestic opponents. There was debate about whether he should visit France if wine were served; a visit to Italy attracted censure because it coincided with opposition (MKOI) activity there; and attempts to obstruct his visit to Germany in mid-2000 involved the arrest of a German national and, later, of participants who had attended a conference in Berlin in January 2000.[53] Nonetheless, these attempts at sabotage (as well as the arrest and sentencing of Iranian Jews charged with spying) have not so far done more than delay the growing rapprochement. The new relationship allows Iran to argue that it is the United States that is isolated. It allows the EU to judge the nature of the regime better and, when necessary, to make its point firmly: e.g., in reminding Iran of its obligations regarding human rights or under the Non-Proliferation Treaty.

Khatami has improved relations with Iran's immediate neighbours and European states, diminishing the isolation felt by Iranians before his presidency. In neither case have the improved relations come at the cost of departures from Iran's national interests. But they have not been easy to achieve, for in each case they entailed a specific and visible departure from a directive of Ayatollah – the Imam – Khomeini: normalisation and ties with Saudi Arabia were specifically banned by Khomeini's last testament, and Rushdie was sentenced under Khomeini's personal *fatwa*. The regime's willingness to follow policies diametrically opposed to Khomeini's dictates indicates a degree of flexibility and pragmatism where its interests are concerned. But this could not have been achieved because of the reformists' power alone. Khatami had the support of Ayatollah Khamene'i behind him.[54]

The improvement in relations remains precarious, being sensitive to issues like Iran's missile and WMD programmes. In the case of the Gulf, the improvement rests on atmospherics, in that it is not buttressed by fundamental agreement on security issues. Further, there is an ambiguity underlying Iran's policies: are improved relations with the GCC and Europe the *precursors* of better relations with the United States (as the reformists believe) or *substitutes* (as the conservatives believe)? Khatami has been cautious, distinguishing his call for a 'dialogue of civilisations' from a 'political dialogue', recognising the red line on this issue drawn by the Supreme Leader. Nonetheless Iran's ties with the EU have expanded considerably with the EU now being Iran's largest trade partner. Regular meetings, consultations and cooperation on a range of issues from drugs to regional stability have become a feature of this new relationship.

Khatami's reform movement has had a significant impact on foreign policy-making in Iran. It has opened the door to debate and criticism in an area once sacrosanct and off-limits, except to a small elite. Pluralising foreign-policy debate, and hence policy-making, is also to demystify it. This implies greater transparency and account-ability. Khatami has certainly achieved this in the debates about relations with the United States, and – more controversially and less directly, as we shall see – about policy toward Israel. In the defence area the influence is less measurable, but, in creating an atmosphere of dialogue and accommodation, he has also suc-ceeded in weakening the alarmist and exclusively military-focused assessments of security.

Chapter 2

Defence and National Security

It is harder to detect a comparable direct impact on defence and national security policies. A number of inter-related reasons account for this: the existence of a national consensus; the low priority the reformists give to national-security issues; divisions among reformists that dilute their influence; the conservatives' tight control over national security, leaving the President powerless to affect it; and similarities between Khatami's and others' views of security. The reasons are not mutually exclusive, and offer a part of the explanation. However, Khatami's more relaxed relations with the Gulf states, and greater overall confidence, have translated into a threat perception lower than the one that was prevalent under his more belligerent predecessors. This chapter looks at Iran's defence doctrine, threat perceptions and strategic approach and an example of its strategy in a particular instance, with particular reference to long-range and SSM missiles. Threat perceptions are by no means uniform, and responses and priorities vary considerably. Although they have been under the exclusive control of the military and their civilian masters, defence doctrine and strategy are not anywhere concisely or authoritatively formulated or registered, thus complicating dissent and debate. Moreover, they are expressed in such very general terms that they defy discussion. Khatami's influence has so far been to defuse the sense of embattlement, rather than to challenge the doctrine directly. However defence doctrine is bound to be influenced by foreign policy, and defence has come to encompass approaches such as confidence-building as well as deterrence. (This becomes potentially more important when we discuss the role of missiles in Iran's strategy in Chapter 3.)

Background
The Consensus: History, War and Ambitions

Iranians are proud nationalists, seeking independence, equality and a greater role, voice and status internationally. The revolution and the war with Iraq have entered folklore as defining moments in the national psyche. They have become imbued, as only myths can, with mystical properties evoked by such terms as 'the imposed war' and the 'Holy Defence' – part of the shared experience of the selfless nation willing to give martyrs for the great cause. Some of the Iranian leadership strive in vain to evoke that era of national mobilisation, unity, sacrifice and obedience, but find that, for all its resonance, this appeal has been overtaken by time.[1]

Iran's defence policy is not confrontational or territorially revisionist; though a defiant country, it is risk-averse. The 'lessons' of the long and traumatic war with Iraq are the basis of defence policy:

- Independence means self-reliance or non-dependence on military supplies from others, hence the need for an indigenous arms industry; and the right to have access to the best technology available;
- Independence also means the right to be treated as an equal and to be taken seriously. Iran is very sensitive about discrimination in general and specifically about discrimination in science and technology as it relates to defence;
- Politically, all this suggests a strategy that is based on *not* counting on world public opinion or UN Security Council intervention;
- Deterrence as well as defence. This implies the ability to retaliate, preferably with the same weapons as the enemy is using ('like-for-like deterrence').
- Emphasis on preparedness – which means no technological surprises from the enemy (and suggests the need to hedge against enemy use of any plausible weapons systems);

- Preparedness for deterrence also requires vigilance (constant exercises) and mobility.

These assumptions or precepts guide the totality of Iran's defence posture. Most Iranians subscribe to them, and they are not seen as questionable, let alone contentious.

Reformists

Unlike foreign policy, which has been discussed in election campaigns, defence policy as such does not figure greatly, if at all, in the national debate. Consequently, expertise in this area is lacking, and this insulates defence policy from intelligent criticism or commentary. Furthermore, it is not a priority issue for the reformers, who are preoccupied with the immediate, pressing domestic needs of the people. For a reformist coalition not given to discussing the issues, devising a common defence platform different from the existing national one might prove a divisive exercise. Still, elements of the thinking of some reformists are clear: they would rely less on missiles and deterrence (shorthand for military might) and more on political reform and a form of 'co-operative security'.[2]

Establishment politicians have not been above playing politics with defence issues; Rafsanjani attributed Iran's 'successful' defence sector to clerical management of the country.[3] What is still lacking in Iran is the ability to discuss defence impartially and dispassionately, and the absence of a historical tradition of debating these issues makes the task harder. Questions are framed in terms of threats and necessities, not in terms of a range of alternative responses, each with a relative cost attached. Issues can quickly take on a factional or nationalist flavour, which impedes rational discussion. Regimes throughout the region seek to hold on to exclusive control of the discussion of defence issues by appropriating the word 'national security', using it indiscriminately and broadly in an effort to fend off challenges to their monopoly.[4] An important question is how the establishment would respond to intelligent criticisms of defence policy, should they emerge.

Opacity in Defence Decision-making

As the *Majlis* has become more assertive, it has spoken up on issues to do with foreign policy, and this will, in time, affect defence policy as well, especially insofar as funding is concerned. Nonetheless, given the closed nature of current Iranian decision-making on national security policy, the analyst must resort to intelligent extrapolation, inference, analogy and speculation. Decision-making in defence is no more transparent than in the programmes for Iran's (alleged) weapons of mass destruction. Formally, the Supreme National Security Council (SNSC) is the institution that co-ordinates decisions affecting national security. It includes the senior military and guards commanders, the Minister of Defence (Ali Shamkhani), the Supreme Leader, the President (nominal head of the SNSC), the Head of the Expediency Council (Rafsanjani), the Secretary of the Council (Hasan Rowhani) and the former Guards Commander (Mohsen Reza'i) among others. Common positions are sought on most issues (or crises) considered to need co-ordination, such as the confrontation with the Taliban in 1998, or the formulation of policy on the islands disputed with Abu Dhabi.[5] (See Appendix.)

Decisions on defence and the monitoring, financing, etc., of on-going defence programmes are multi-year activities. Yet over time the leadership has changed, as has the composition of the SNSC, and the Presidency and even military chiefs have come and gone. It is a reasonable inference that decision-making in the most sensitive areas (missiles, nuclear, biological and chemical weapons) is limited to a small group of people who have survived the changes, though sometimes changing their hats along the way. An educated guess would put the core of those tasked with dealing with sensitive defence issues as: Khamene'i, Rafsanjani, Reza'i, Shamkhani, Ali Shahbazi and possibly Rowhani. As in most things in Iran, the informal prevails over the formal. A small group, comprising trusted elements, assures the continuity that long-range programmes presuppose and limits the risk of leaks. Evidence for this is necessarily inconclusive, but the inference can be drawn from the way in which it is usually the same people who make public comments about defence issues, even in cases where their official positions entail no formal defence responsibility (e.g. Reza'i and, especially, Rafsanjani).[6] This circle in all probability does not currently include Khatami and his reformist advisers, but how long this will remain the case is uncertain.

Lack of Presidential Control

Defence Minister Ali Shamkhani pointedly declared in mid-1999, at the height of student demonstrations that shook the regime, that Iran's security policies were not subject to alteration because of domestic (political) changes.[7] He was not challenged on this, despite the implication that there was no room for debate on what Iran's security policies ought to be. The comment also reflected another reality: that, while the President names the Defence Minister and Guards Minister, promotions in both military organisations rest with the Supreme Leader, as does effective control of the Islamic Revolutionary Guard Corps (IRGC).

The IRGC's principal mission is differentiated from the regular military by its focus on assuring security against internal threats. This makes national security ambiguous (Security of the revolution? Regime security?) and leaves the IRGC's mission open to abuse and selective, self-interested definition.

The conservatives have not failed to use the Guards to act as their partisan police force to enforce decisions made by the judiciary, which they dominate, or for intelligence purposes in their struggle with the reformists.[8] However, it is by no means clear that the Revolutionary Guards, especially the rank and file, are all supporters of the hard-liners. It seems more likely that they reflect the broader divisions in the country itself.[9]

Khatami and Defence

On three occasions in 2000, President Khatami complained publicly that he lacked the means to implement policies. 'As the person responsible for national security', he said in August, he did not have the 'necessary tools'; in December he observed, 'I must admit that after three years and a half in the presidency I am aware that the head of state does not have adequate authority to do his job'; and in November he noted that he lacked the authority to implement the constitution.[10] Because of their potential for use in the political and social spectrum, defence or national security policy (defined broadly) are unlikely to be relinquished early or voluntarily by the conservative opponents of the reform movement. Assuming he wishes to do so, Khatami's ability to direct (as opposed to influence) defence policy, will therefore remain limited.

But how far does Khatami's vision of Iran's defence and security differ from that of the conservatives? To judge from his public pronouncements, not much. He has argued the need for 'strong and capable' armed forces whose equipment 'must be one of the top priorities' of the country and whose capabilities would manifest Iran's 'pride and authority'. While insisting on Iran's peaceful intentions, he has strongly denounced the foreign military presence in the Persian Gulf as illegitimate and a 'threat to security'.[11]

Khatami has supported deterrence as the guarantor of Iran's success in other areas, including economic and political development, and sees this as requiring peacetime strength: 'we have to be strong so that the enemy does not even think about committing aggression against us' and 'we have no choice but to have a strong military capability'. Khatami shares the pride of others in Iran's defence industries and in its right to seek the best technology available for it. He also argues that all Iran's 'scientific, defensive, and technical potential' is available to the Muslim world.

Khatami has pointed to Israel as the greatest regional threat, singling out its nuclear, chemical and biological weapons arsenal: 'It can use it at any moment in order to threaten neighbouring, Arab, Islamic and independent countries in the world'. At the same time he has insisted that Iran opposes the proliferation of all weapons of mass destruction:

> *Today, owning weapons of mass destruction is a costly affair and a threat to the region and the countries that hold these weapons. It also prevents the use of resources and capabilities for the benefit of the progress and welfare of the people.*
>
> *At the same time banning these weapons will only work if there is no differentiation or discrimination.*[12]

The defence industry, and the unfettered right of access to science and technology, are key themes and components of Iran's defence policies. To Westerners, these sometimes sound like code words for the development of technology for possible weapons use, whereas to Iranians discrimination and restrictions on the supply of 'dual-capable' technologies appear as a thinly disguised means to keep countries that show independence backward and weak. The government equates scientific progress with an advanced defence sector, and sees both as essential attributes of status for important powers like Iran. This is reflected in the government's sponsorship of the sciences in the defence sector (such as through the Aerospace Industries Organization) and the absence of a comparable private or market sector.

Khatami is no less keen than his political competitors to rely on military power to guarantee security and to enhance it through access to advanced technology. Where he is somewhat different is in the desire to reassure other states (with the exception of Israel) of Iran's peaceful intentions.

> *We have been able to develop our defence industry. It is indeed defensive, because we have no aggressive intentions towards anyone. We are trying to develop this industry correctly and without alarming anyone.*[13]

Iran's Defence Doctrine

Iran's defence doctrine has been formed by a mixture of elements – lessons learned, assumptions about threats, available resources, and the values and principles held by the leadership. However, since there is no authoritative or comprehensive expression of this doctrine, it has to be inferred from a mixture of sources: public declarations, force structure, procurement patterns, military expenditures and allocations, and the type and the nature of military exercises undertaken. (Where nuclear, chemical and biological weapons are concerned, Iran denies either possession or intent, so there is naturally no clear expression of a doctrine. Any intention to acquire WMD thus has to be inferred from analogies and by informed speculation, making them at best, educated guesses.)

Iran's defence doctrine has evolved considerably from the romantic focus on 'defence in depth' and 'the nation in arms' in which revolutionary zeal and élan were considered substitutes for training, hierarchy, organisation and equipment. Iran now focuses on training and exercises, and attaches more importance to deterrence in addition to defence. It emphasises self-sufficiency but also seeks access to advanced technology as a form of insurance policy. This is true in the conventional area through the reliance on missiles; it may also be true in relation to a nuclear-weapons option.

It is rare for self-reliance to be sought for economic reasons, or because the arms required are not available abroad. Generally, under self-reliance, domestic arms are costlier and inferior to the imported product.[14] However other values, such as independence (or reduced vulnerability to interruptions of supply), are at stake. Insistence on an indigenous defence industry entails certain consequences. In Iran's case it has led to a practical emphasis on what is achievable, and what its leaders consider important compensatory systems, i.e. missiles.

Iran's defence doctrine, with its focus on preparedness, mobility and retaliatory capacity to create deterrence, is unexceptional. Frequent military exercises are intended to improve readiness, mobility and combined-arms operations and to send a political message that acts as a deterrent. At the same time, Khatami's détente policy towards the Gulf states is intended to reassure the GCC of Iran's peaceful intentions.

Iran has long land borders with Iraq to the west and Afghanistan to the east, combined with limited airlift capability, and a capacity for storing materiel in multiple locations that is constrained by climate and resource limitations. Hence, its ability to mobilise and redeploy troops quickly over distances is important. This capacity, tested notably in autumn 1998 against the Taliban, appears to have improved, probably as a result of these frequent exercises.

However, as most threats are not seen as emanating from the ground, Iran's research and development focus has been on equipment related to the air force or the navy, with electronics as a priority.[15] Nonetheless Iran seeks 'all round independence and self-sufficiency' as a priority.[16]

The threat level is seen as particularly high in the Persian Gulf. This perception stems from several sources. First, the inherent importance of the waterway for oil exports and essential imports, and its vulnerability to disruption. Second, the military presence of the US, which outmatches Iran's capabilities, and which is a reminder of the US attacks on Iranian ships and oil rigs in 1987–88; this is underscored by the poor relations with the US since 1979, which has occasionally given rise to talk of attacks on Iran. These concerns give Iran reason to consider how it might, under crisis conditions, use its military forces to deny the US control of the sea, and complicate its access to the Gulf. (Short of crisis conditions, Iran clearly has a vital interest in keeping the waterway safe and open.) To deny the US sea control, Iran has acquired mines, missiles and fast patrol boats for use within the Gulf, and submarines (3 *Kilo*-class bought from Russia since 1994) to operate outside it.

Threat Perceptions

Iran's strategic environment is characterised by instability and diversity: unstable neighbours, low-level conflicts and the legacies associated with them, notably refugees. Despite endemic problems around its land borders (war and conflict in Iraq; a restive and divided Kurdish population there and in Turkey; continuing tension between Azerbaijan and Armenia, volatility in nearby Georgia and Tajikistan, and civil war in Afghanistan), this generalised instability does not translate into a serious security problem. The situation is diffuse; it requires attention and resources, but it does not constitute an urgent, overwhelming threat to Iran's territorial integrity or existence. Iran thus has multiple *concerns* but no existential *threats*. This is suggested by the tendency, when pressed, to talk of 'cultural threats' rather than 'life and death threats'.[17] Some reformists insist that the major threats are in fact domestic and should be recognised as such: 'We should pay more attention to domestic issues and find solutions under [the] complicated conditions of today and avoid putting the blame on events outside the borders'.[18]

In fact Iranian leaders often refer to Iran's fortunate strategic position as an 'island of stability'.[19] Iran's concerns are about low-level violence spilling over into its territory from the Kurdish areas, from the opposition MKOI in Iraq and the drug-smugglers, and about refugees from violence on all its frontiers. Few of these concerns call for sophisticated weapons, let alone weapons of mass destruction. In the case of the eastern borders near Afghanistan and Pakistan, the need is for mobility, solid borders and policing. Relative to most of its neighbours, Iran is in a fortunate position.

In the north, Iran has cultivated good relations with Russia, reflecting a range of overlapping interests – including opposition to NATO and the extension of US power into the Caucasus, and hence a certain distrust of Turkey. Iran sees Russia as an important source of arms and (nuclear) technology and a potential diplomatic counterweight to the US. Russia sees Iran as a useful market, a state that can help stabilise the periphery (e.g. by not creating a nuisance over Chechnya) and as a potential lever in a spoiler strategy. Iran has not allowed differences over pipeline routes or division of the Caspian's waters to upset relations. Moreover, this relationship shows signs of becoming more important with the expansion of Iran's arms purchases since late 2000 and the absence of any meaningful rapprochement with the US. At the same time, though, as Russia's own relations with the United States improve, Moscow may become more careful in its dealings with Tehran, especially over technology transfers.

Since 1991, Iran has sought to influence neighbouring states in the Caspian region by emphasising cultural and historical ties, with little regard to religious or sectarian affiliation (a notable example being Iran's support for the Armenians against fellow-Shi'i Azeris). In general, Iran has preferred to play the peacemaker, as in Tajikistan, taking a conservative position with regard to frontier changes. The priority has been to cultivate neighbouring states as part of Khatami's détente policy, which has obvious parallels with his Gulf policy. Economic cooperation is envisaged, including in the energy sector and notably with Turkmenistan. Investment is, however, constrained by the state of Iran's economy and its limited access to foreign investment.

To the east, Iran's security is more problematic. Here spill-overs from wars in Afghanistan have imposed a heavy burden on Iran in hosting a large refugee influx (up to 2 million). More recently, since 1996, this has been compounded by the rise of the Taliban, who insisted on persecuting the Shia population in the

Hazarajat region as heretics. Iran, which has long insisted that the solution to the Afghan civil war is a multi-ethnic coalition, was faced with the domination of the Sunni and Pashtan Taliban (sponsored by Pakistan) who, in persecuting the Shia Hazaras, directly challenge Iran's claim as the leader and defender of the Shia world. After Iranian diplomats were massacred by the Taliban in Herat in autumn 1998, Iran mobilised its forces, but refrained from a military reprisal. Besides targeting the Shia minority, hosting terrorists like Osama bin Laden (thus putting Iran and the US on the same side on at least one issue) and prolonging the civil war, the Taliban posed another kind of danger: that of instability and lawlessness spilling into Iran. Drug cultivation and violence increased, with smuggling into Iran growing apace. Clashes on the borders with smugglers and kidnappers – a low-grade security issue – has become a near daily occurrence, resulting in the death of some 3,000 security officials in recent years. For the first time, drugs have become a social issue in Iran, the Central Asian and the Gulf states: a matter of security concern for regimes as well as a basis for greater regional cooperation.

Relations with Pakistan, which used to be warm, have deteriorated. In part this is due to Pakistan's sponsorship of the Taliban and to the increase in sectarian violence targeted at the Shia minority in Pakistan itself. In part, it is due to Iran's suspicion that Pakistan is itself becoming Talibanised. Pakistan's decision to cross the nuclear threshold in 1998 also gave Iran cause to consider the wider implications of nuclear rivalry beyond the subcontinent. Iran has reason to seek a stabilisation of relations between Islamabad and New Delhi, for security reasons as well as for the prospect of finding a market for its future gas exports to the subcontinent, which would be routed overland by pipeline. In the short term, the concern is that Pakistan could become a further problem if it assumes more of the attributes of a failing state, with a concomitant spill-over of instability into its neighbours. Coordination between the two countries on a post-Taliban Afghanistan is necessary if competition is to be minimised.

In theory, Iraq is the most obvious traditional security threat to Iran. It remains ambitious and keen to retain and increase its capability in the area of weapons of mass destruction. (Ironically, sanctions aimed at this capability have also eroded Iraq's *conventional* military means, thus in the short term increasing its reliance on WMD as a substitute.) With a record of miscalculation and aggression, Saddam Hussein's Iraq remains a volatile force in the region. Iraq has used WMD and ascribes its victory over Iran in 1988 in part to these. Continued testing of missiles like the *al-Sammoud* in mid-2000 suggests continuing interest. It should be recalled that Iraq's original decision to seek such weapons was motivated as much for deployment against Iran as against Israel.[20] Whether because it fears Iran's intentions or seeks revenge, Iraq may well in future decide to use these WMD again. Iraq and Iran have exchanged accusations that each secretly possesses weapons of mass destruction.[21]

Differences between Iran and Iraq (notably over borders, the Algiers Accord of 1975 regulating these, the status of prisoners of war, war reparations, etc.) have still to be settled. Iran and Iraq host each other's opposition groups (MKOI and SCIRI), who undertake attacks and assassinations against the other state. These attacks, whose tempo has not abated in recent years, are punctuated by Iranian retaliatory strikes against Mujahiddin bases in Iraq, often using missiles.

Iraq has to be concerned about an Iran that might be motivated by revenge, and, to counter this, might seek a pre-emptive war. This might be considered seriously if Iraq felt it could catch Iran unprepared, or thought it could isolate Iran in the region by depicting the conflict as an Arab–Iranian war. Neither eventuality appears probable at present, as Iran remains vigilant and has improved ties with the GCC states. Also, Iraq remains subject to containment and embargo, thus limiting its deteriorating conventional capabilities. Hence, although Iran does not see an Iraqi threat as a major danger in the short to medium term, Iraq nonetheless remains its most serious overall national-security threat. Iran has limited its response to increasing the readiness and mobility of its forces and building a deterrent (first, by acquiring missiles and, second, by developing a full spectrum of WMD as a future weapons option). Sooner or later, though, Iraq will have to be reintegrated into the region, and consideration will need to be given to regional approaches to arms control – and these approaches will have to consider more than one category of weapon.

Of all Iran's neighbours, it would seem that Turkey is the most important. Yet it is also the most neglected. Iranian leaders seem to take Turkey for granted, appear to have little knowledge of that country and give it less attention than it warrants. Iran has no bilateral disputes with Turkey, no border disputes, and there is no historical irredentism or animosity to complicate relations. A common orientation during the Cold War was disrupted by Iran's revolution – which, with its emphasis on Islam, disturbed secular Turkey; after some initial attempts at subversion in the 1980s (to which Turkey under-reacted) the IRI cut back on its provocative actions. The possibility of cooperation on energy has been mooted but remains largely dormant, due to financial considerations. Iran and Turkey have not become drawn into the kind of competition in Central Asia and the Caucasus that some people anticipated in the early 1990s; though they differ on the pipeline politics of the region, and each wants a large slice of transit fees, they also co-operate. Neither has an interest in stirring up regional conflict, and they share an interest in the territorial integrity of a contained Iraq.

In recent years Turkey has been seen as the vanguard of an expansive NATO that seeks to extend to the Caspian region, a notion fed by some Azeri politicians. More serious, though, is the growth of Israeli–Turkish military cooperation, which some Iranians see as a prelude to an Israeli military attack on Iran's defence facilities.[22] In what seems to have been a response, Iran started to support the militant Marxist Kurdish PKK group. This in turn led Turkey in mid-1999 to make armed incursions into Iranian territory, which was allegedly being used as a sanctuary. Iranian objections resulted in the formation of a joint security commission to study and discuss issues pertaining to border security. Turkey has renewed criticism of Iranian intervention in its internal affairs.

Whether Iran's policy of putting pressure on Turkey enjoys support from all factions in Iran is unclear. What is evident is that a conciliatory response draws criticism from hardliners. One journal asked, 'What can possibly justify so much leniency toward a state which is effectively acting as the regional puppet of the Zionist regime?' It went on to refer to Turkey as 'a third grade military dictatorship which is bootlicking the outsiders, including the Zionist occupiers of holy Quds'.[23]

Although Iran's relations with Turkey need attention, however critical Iran may be of Israel's treatment of the Palestinians, it does not intend to take a direct part in that dispute, and so differences with Turkey do not logically extend as far as military conflict. Similarly, although Iran's development of long-range missiles should be seen primarily as a response to its *proximate* defence needs, rather than as strategic weapons aimed at Israel, Iran's indirect support for Israel's foes and Tehran's harsh rhetoric make such an interpretation difficult (and less plausible) for Israel. Tensions between Iran and Israel and Iranian rhetoric, in turn make improving Iranian ties with Turkey more difficult.

Iran's principal strategic preoccupations are two states which are not neighbours: Israel and the US.[24]

Although Iran and Israel have no direct bilateral dispute, conflict could occur as a result of:

i. a spiral of exchanges and blows stemming from events surrounding Iran's support for forces opposed to Israel – e.g. Hezbollah's activities; or
ii. a decision by Israel to seek to prevent Iran's development of nuclear or other WMD by a military strike; IRGC commander Mohsen Reza'i referred to the possibility that Israel might provoke the US into starting a war. As discussed below Iran sees missiles as playing an important role here.

The other major threat is seen to be the United States. The nearby US military presence, together with repeated US air and cruise-missile strikes against adversaries in Iraq, Sudan and Afghanistan, suggests a power able to inflict punishment at will. In Iran's view, pretexts for punishing Iran are not lacking, so it needs a strategy for deterring such threats; denial of control of Persian Gulf waters is one aspect of this strategy.

Iran's Strategic Approach

Iran's strategy is neither highly evolved nor clearly enunciated. However it is based on a clear understanding of Iran's weaknesses and a degree of experience gained in the war with Iraq. The strategy also reflects a 'national style', which is indirect and elliptical, rather than direct. I shall first outline the elements of the strategy and then discuss a case where it has been applied.

Iranian leaders appear to have a conception of proportional or minimal deterrence based on the assumption that deterring a more powerful state depends on the ability to raise the costs to that state of a particular action, thus making it unprofitable. This does not require equivalent capabilities: effective means to impose a penalty and raise the costs are enough. Iran has sought to make clear to an aggressor (it is chiefly the US that it has in mind) that an attack on Iran would entail:

- a certain response, but not necessarily one that the attacker expects;
- Iranian willingness to take casualties;
- a wider conflict in, and possibly outside, the region;
- prolongation of the conflict (i.e., Iran would decide when to end it);
- probable escalation (i.e., the attacker should not count on a proportional response).

Some of these approaches were tried in the war with Iraq, without total success. Now, however, Iran has the means – mines, submarines, missiles – to make the threat of retaliation much more persuasive. All these themes and threats were used in the case discussed below.

Iran's Response to the Threat of US Military Action after Al Khobar: an Example of Deterrence

The Iranian leadership expected a US attack in 1996–97 because of US suspicions that Iran had been responsible for the June 1996 bombing of a US military base in Saudi Arabia in which 19 US servicemen had been killed. Israeli sources soon linked the bombing with Hezbollah and observed that it 'will greatly increase the chance of a US military strike on Iran even before the US presidential elections in November'.[25]

Outgoing President Rafsanjani, in his farewell address (August 1997), alluded to both Iran's activities and to the threat indirectly:

*We have powerful enemies, the USA, Israel and other
countries. I still have my concerns about this. We have to be
careful in the future. In our foreign policy we should act in
a way that could achieve our objectives and maintain our
ideals without seriously damaging our country.*[26]

President Khatami later (in 2001) alluded to the episode saying
that when he came to office 'Iran faced a serious military threat'.
He said that since then, as a result of Iran's defence programmes,
'It would be very costly ... to launch an attack on the Islamic
Republic of Iran today'.[27]

Iran's reaction to that threat is indicative. The Supreme
Leader, Khamene'i, depicting the world as a jungle where might is
right, concluded that to resist bullying 'a state must be able to claw
the face of the aggressor and make it regret its aggression'.[28] Iran
could not defeat the US, but might deter it, or make it think twice.

Cultivating a willingness to suffer and absorb costs was
considered important in the war with Iraq and has been revived as
an aspect of deterrence. Iran's willingness to take casualties is
assumed to be a source of strength; while (assumed) US unwillingness to do so is something to be played upon. The Guards
Commander, Mohsen Reza'i, saw Iran's 'culture of martyrdom' as
a source of power. While not seeking conflict, Iran would turn the
Persian Gulf into a 'slaughterhouse for them' if the US launched an
attack.[29]

Widening the war was an explicit Iranian threat. 'We will
disregard all restrictions ... throughout the Persian Gulf up to the
Sea of Oman.'[30] Reviving the phrase from the Gulf War, the
Supreme Leader warned: 'Our insecurity means insecurity for the
region ... the region as a whole, the enemies of our nation in
particular, those sitting in a glass house will become more in-
secure'.[31] Rafsanjani later observed that Iran had been restrained
vis-à-vis Iraq in 1980–88: 'At that time we were considerate of the
situation in the interests of our neighbours lest the war might
spread to other parts of the region ...'.[32] And the Guards Commander, Rahim-Safavi, warned that Iran could respond 'in any part of
the world' and would react 'immediately, effectively and deci-
sively' to any form of aggression. He also suggested that Iran's

determination *to prolong* the war with Iraq from 1982 to 1988 had been to punish the aggressor, 'to exact a price for the aggression'.[33]

The US did not pursue the military option against Iran, for its own reasons. The evidence was inconclusive. The emergence of the Khatami Presidency and the reform movement suggested possible moderation in Iran, which might be endangered by an attack. And US regional allies, above all Saudi Arabia and Israel, were against a US military strike because they might be the target of an Iranian 'retaliatory' response. Whether the US had been deterred by Iran is difficult to demonstrate. But Iran's willingness to retaliate and raise the costs of an attack had surely been a consideration. Its readiness to widen, prolong and escalate the crisis and to threaten regional stability and the security of key allies makes the contemplation of a 'limited strike' a nonsense – such a strike would entail a war, and that raises the stakes politically and acts to deter the initiator of the exchanges in all but the most vital cases.

Iran has embraced the concept of deterrence and sought to buttress it through military exercises, self-sufficiency and the acquisition of missiles, whether anti-ship or surface-to-surface. There is little evidence of dissent on the broad lines of this approach.

Chapter 3

Iran's Missile Programme

Iran's missile and nuclear weapons programmes are both controversial and potentially destabilising regionally. Additionally, the reformers' influence on both is limited, because these are areas of national security controlled by the hard-liners. There, however, the resemblance between the two programmes ends. The nuclear weapons programme – which Iran denies – is clandestine, illegal and potentially subject to political debate, contention and reversal. The missile programme is proceeding openly, under no legal prohibitions or constraints, and subject to little domestic political scrutiny, debate or questioning. This makes it a live, not a theoretical, issue in the current security of the region, and this chapter will examine both its aims and its impact on affected regional states. Iran makes no apologies for seeking a missile capability, considering it an essential part of its deterrent strategy. Yet, the acquisition of such a capability is inherently ambiguous, as are Iran's statements about its intended uses. In this connection the impact on relations with Israel assume importance, making it necessary to discuss measures that Iran might take to reduce the insecurity that accompanies the development of missile forces.

Missiles in Iranian National Security

Iran equates missiles with advanced weapons, precision and deterrence. It seeks 'a deterrent force' and 'arms with effective deterrent capabilities', which, together with 'defence preparedness', are the basis of defence planning.[1] Iran was not the first among its immediate neighbours to acquire missiles (Iraq was), nor the first to seek long-range missiles (Saudi Arabia and later Iraq led the way). In the wider region, Israel has had missiles (the *Jericho*-2) with the range to reach Iran since 1986. However, Iran's emphasis on the importance of missiles raises the question of what role they play in its defence and strategy more generally.

Iran launched a crash programme to obtain missiles from Libya, Syria, North Korea and China during the Iran–Iraq war, when its air force was virtually grounded by a US-led arms embargo ('Operation Staunch'). The unimpeded and liberal use of missiles by Iraq, especially against cities, left a strong impression on the Iranian leadership (and played a role in Tehran's decision to accept the cease-fire in July 1988). Missiles seemed to offer a way of compensating for the largely grounded (and aging) air force, originally US-supplied but now deprived of access to spare parts or system upgrades.

With the end of the war with Iraq, Iranian officials, drawing on recent experience (as well as their principles) saw missiles as a means of defence that was accessible to them. Unlike an air force (which would inevitably be foreign-supplied, costly to train and maintain, need frequent upgrading and involve dependence on foreign sources), missiles might become the foundation of a dom-estic defence industry, giving Iran relative autonomy in security planning. In addition, for a country that had not excelled militarily in the recent war, missiles appeared to offer a possible and painless remedy. While not exactly 'equalisers' (they do not eliminate weaknesses in Iran's conventional capabilities), missiles provide a painless path to raw destructive power and, by effectively decou-pling the ability to hurt an adversary from the capability to prosecute a war effectively, provide a shortcut to effective deter-rence. As substitutes for air power, they might not be as flexible (e.g. recallable) or carry comparable payloads, but they could be relatively sure of penetrating enemy defences, would not require pilots and could be made secure through mobility and conceal-ment. All these characteristics strongly commended them to Iran's post-war defence planners.

Many of these points were made by Rafsanjani while still president, after reports of purchases of missiles from China and

North Korea. He observed that the purchases were within a purely defensive framework and would not be used to attack anyone; that after the experience with Iraq, Iran needed a defence capability and that 'a country like Iran cannot give up the missile industry'.[2]

Iran's 'right' to scientific research – to have access to advanced technologies in order to create a modern state and economy – and some states' attempts to prevent this is a recurring theme. Such technology includes missiles, and space as well as biological, nuclear and chemical technology and their associated peaceful applications and uses. Missiles have come to be equated with high technology and status, and attempts by some powers to deny this to Iran 'illegally' is seen as only part of a broader strategy of technology-denial on dubious pretexts.[3] In a wide-ranging, authoritative, speech on this theme covering biological, chemical and nuclear technology, Rafsanjani also mentioned missiles, noting that 'Iran has a right to maintain its defensive capabilities' and that, as a result of the war with Iraq, Iran had come to realise that missiles

> *were vital to us. We therefore pursued the matter scientifically. We started from zero. To the same extent that one may have to import spare parts for other industries ...we acquired it the same as other industries. At present Iran is truly a missile manufacturing country and it does not need any other country, neither China, Russia nor anywhere else.*
>
> *Hence Iran is impervious to US-led efforts to restrict technology to Iran.*[4]

President Khatami has shown no signs of dissenting from these views, observing that Iran's military programmes are 'defensive in nature' and that Iran has the right 'to gain access to scientific facilities'.[5] Indeed there is no sign of fundamental disagreement within Iran on defence policies or the assumptions on which they are based. Continuity has therefore been assured for defence programmes, despite political change. After the first *Shihab* tests, Defence Minister Ali Shamkhani observed that defence and security policy was 'not bound by internal policies' and that 'no one would make changes in the strategic security requirements of a country, no matter who is in power'.[6]

Missile Development

Iran has developed a range of missiles. They include short range, surface-to-surface weapons such as *Fazeat* (80–150 km range), *Fadjr* and *Zelzal* (200 km range/600 kg payload), as well as coastal-based anti-ship missiles and cruise missiles, and Iran now *claims* to be nearly self sufficient in manufacturing capability.[7] It has also expressed interest in the Russian S-300 air-defence system, which can track and destroy six low-flying cruise missiles or aircraft at one time. This technology could be relevant to Iran's missile programme.[8]

Our principal area of interest is in Iran's ballistic missile programme. The *Shihab*-3, tested in July 1998, is 53 ft long and believed to have a range of 1,300 km. The Defence Minister announced that *Shihab*-3 would be mass-produced but its successors, *Shihab*-4 and -5, with greater range and payloads would (only) be used for launching orbiting telecommunications satellites. In February 2000 Iran claimed to be self-sufficient in the production of solid fuel for rockets. A second missile test was announced in July 2000, and in September a test was announced of the *Shihab*-3D, combining a solid and a liquid propellant (Iran's first solid-fuel type).[9]

In mid-1999, Iran announced its expectation of launching a satellite communications system, the *Zowreh*, within two years and stated that it 'reserves the right to make peaceful use of space'. At the same time, officials have insisted that Iran does not seek a military capability beyond that of the *Shihab*-3, implying that all future developments in this field are intended for peaceful space-based applications, such as space launch vehicles and satellite guidance systems.[10]

In mid-2000 it was announced that the IRGC air force had set up five ballistic-missile units. This confirmed the impression that these weapons would be in the hands of the elements of the regime that were assumed to be the most politically reliable, although, compared to regular military (air force), less technically proficient.

Doctrine

Iran's proclaimed peaceful intentions and the fact that its missile programme is a *response* to those of other states, does not reassure the United States and Israel. They see *any* increase in Iran's military capabilities as inherently dangerous, and especially any increase in capabilities that could be used as a cover for, or contribute to, the development of WMD. According to this view, given Iran's animosity and 'tendency to lie, cheat and obfuscate', a defence programme ostensibly couched in terms of 'legitimate defence needs' could easily be intended for more aggressive purposes.

It is important to assess to what extent Iran's missile programme represents a considered part of its defence doctrine, whether that doctrine is coherent and what its implications are for Iranian behaviour. It has been seen that the desire to possess missiles and missile technology started from necessity and evolved into a dogma that saw this as a 'right', at once important for purposes of being 'modern', and at the same time providing a weapons system potentially useful to states determined to be independent and effective.

How are missiles seen and what are the assumptions about their utility? The inconsistency of Iranian statements makes it difficult to be sure. The mixed signals sent out in hard-to-reconcile public declarations may indicate differences of view or, more likely, an incoherence that stems from lack of disciplined analysis and discussion of the issues. It certainly exemplifies a tendency of the current regime to 'want to have it both ways'.[11] The effect is to foster uncertainty over whether Iran sees missiles as primarily for deterrence or for something more (specifically offensive purposes).

Although Iran originally sought to acquire missiles during the conflict with Iraq, and this has remained the rationale for their acquisition, few references are now made to an actual or potential Iraqi threat as a continuing incentive for developing missiles. The focus has now shifted to Israel. In part this reflects a belief that Israel, potentially or actually, constitutes a military threat to Iran; partly it is a result of Iran's development of these weapons (see below). But Israel serves an important function in serving to justify Iran's controversial development of advanced (and unconventional) weapons with potential regional impact. For now, the missiles are offered in a common cause, and the Israeli focus diverts attention from Iran's programmes and avoids any Iranian–Arab split that might result if Iran emphasised the Iraqi rationale for the development of WMD. Hence Iran seeks to argue that the missiles are both for defence and deterrence *and* for the benefit of the wider Islamic and Arab world.

Iranian officials have usually referred to missiles as intended for deterrence and reserved for defence and retaliation, rather than for initiating hostilities. However, they have also sought to depict them as intended for the defence of fellow Muslims and Arabs. This inconsistency has been prevalent since Rafsanjani noted in 1996 that missiles were seen within a 'purely defensive framework. We have no hostile intentions toward anyone ... . We will not use the missiles to attack any country'. But he then added that some states play up the 'Iranian danger' and minimise that of Israel, yet 'if the Arabs and Muslims still consider Israel their real enemy, as in the past, they must view Iran as their *strategic backyard* [emphasis added] and must seek co-operation with us'.[12]

After the first test of the *Shihab*-3 missile, statements emphasising its deterrent function multiplied, but without dispelling the ambiguity. Iran's defence policy, said the defence minister, was based on 'increasing the capacity to deter'. He went on to say that, despite the hostility of others, Iran enjoyed good relations with the Gulf countries, and that 'our capability is theirs and their capability is ours'. He amplified this by saying that 'at least in the mid-term, the neighbouring countries do not pose any threat'.[13] Other senior officials, too, depicted the development of missiles as an enhancement of Iran's 'deterrent ability', and Shamkhani noted that the aim of developing missiles is to strengthen defence 'within a framework of the principle of deterrence' and their range, accuracy and destructive power makes missiles 'military equipment that, with minimum cost, can have maximum effects on our deterrent capabilities'.[14]

Defence Minister Shamkhani took pains to emphasise that Iran's 'principal defence policy is to enhance its deterrent capability'. Iran's strategy was based on minimising the effects of a first strike while maintaining a robust second strike capability, with which it could conclude hostilities. However, he added: 'Both the Islamic and Arab countries will definitely welcome the advent of this capability and will consider it part of their own.'[15] Such vague comments about sharing Iran's capabilities with neighbours have stretched the rationale for acquiring missiles. The most expansive being the suggestion by a senior Guards official that '*Shehab*-3 is a tool for defending the Muslim '*ummah* and the oppressed nations'.[16] No doubt reflecting the consensus developed in the SNSC, President Khatami took much the same line, depicting Israel as the great regional threat, stressing that the danger stemmed from Israel's nuclear weapons (not Iran's missiles) and calling for solidarity among Muslims.[17]

Iran's statements have not stopped there. The leadership has argued that Iranian missile production would ultimately cause Israel to cut back on its huge weapons arsenal; that the *Shihab*-3 would not land in any 'Islamic country'; and that Iran was developing missiles for self-defence against 'nuclear armed countries near Iran'.[18] Iranian leaders have also been unable to resist bragging: e.g. when Rafsanjani asserted that Iran's progress on missiles was giving 'Israel nightmares'.[19]

Specific doctrine about actual employment beyond defensive and retaliatory use against military targets has been lacking. On a number of occasions the defence minister has hinted that the missile capability should deter any (pre-emptive) attack from Israel against Iranian facilities, such as the nuclear plant at Bushire, and in 1998 he said that Iran would use missiles against Israel if it attacked this installation. This was followed by a statement from the Hezbollah leadership in Lebanon suggesting that, in case of an Israeli attack against Iran, Iran could respond with attacks on Israel from Lebanese territory – a statement later retracted.[20] That episode was suggestive in underscoring that, pending the development of a reliable long-range missile, Iran could arrange a kind of interim deterrent by using Hezbollah as a strategic ally and launching pad, arming it with missiles with enough range to reach deep into Israel.

In another similar episode, which required clarification and retraction, Shamkhani suggested that Iran 'would not leave [Syria and Lebanon] alone in the face of an Israeli attack' and that Iran's 'response will be astonishing and unexpected.' He also increased the deliberate ambiguity by remarking, 'You do not say everything you know, and you do not write everything you say.'[21] Shamkhani's most recent statement goes beyond defence and retaliation and, *if missiles are being referred to*, suggests an attempt to extend deterrence beyond Iran's national territory.

Has Iran expanded its ideas about the utility of missiles as its programmes have developed? Is it indeed official policy to seek to extend a security umbrella, and deterrence, beyond Iran's national territory? The evidence is mixed. Statements are inconsistent, with frequent reference to the deterrent functions of missiles, comments about (and condemnation of) Israel, reassuring statements to neighbours, and defiant statements aimed at the West about the right to technology and security. The inconsistencies, pronouncements and opacity give rise to understandable alarm in Israel. But, against this, Iran's record is one of relative realism and pragmatism, together with an aversion to risk.[22]

Israel and Iran's Missile Programme

No state has been more concerned about Iran's development of ballistic missiles than Israel, and none has done as much to seek to prevent, retard and neutralise it. In the context of overlapping rivalries and multiple strategic axes, missile proliferation increases uncertainties in several ways. First, the parallel development of biological, chemical and (in some cases) nuclear weapons programmes raises the question of whether these missiles may be armed with such warheads. Statements from various governments have suggested that these programmes are seen as ways of offsetting Israel's (still undeclared but generally assumed) nuclear weapons capability. The WMD programmes are also sometimes depicted as strategic equalisers against Israel's superior conventional weapons. Whether authoritative or not, the emergence of these capabilities, the attempt by some states – notably Egypt (the Mubarak plan) – to trade ratification of the chemical weapons convention for Israel's accession to the Nuclear Non-proliferation Treaty (NPT), serves to blur the threshold of these weapons and obscure their uses. Confusion about the limits and risks of seeking to deter one set of weapons with another creates greater scope for miscalculation. Although some uncertainty lies at the heart of all deterrent relationships, doctrinal confusion (in which postures are adopted for public as much as practical reasons) can lead to misjudgement among adversaries that are not in contact with each other.

The emergence of missile proliferation and the development of WMD hit the region forcefully in 1991 with the Iraqi use of missiles against Israeli cities. Since then their implications for Israel have become clearer. Together, they have:

i.   eroded Israel's strategic depth, bringing distant threats closer and reducing warning times;
ii. challenged Israel's uncontested air superiority and reduced its freedom of action; and hence,
iii. increased the need to buttress deterrence (and defence).

Since the Iraqi missile attacks in 1991, Israel has been alert to signs that potential adversaries might imitate Iraq. In the light of Jewish history and the size of their country, Israelis are especially sensitive to the possible use of WMD warheads mounted on missiles. So far as Iran is concerned, Israeli concern stems from Iran's refusal to recognise the legitimate existence of Israel, in the light of which its development of missiles and WMD must be considered a strategic threat to Israel. In parallel with its missile and WMD programmes there has been a hardening of Iran's position on the Palestine issue, its rejection of the Madrid Peace Process and its encouragement and sponsorship of activist rejectionist groups (discussed below). An alarmed Israel has supported the US policy of 'dual containment' and been in the forefront of states advocating measures to deny Iran access to technology that might be relevant to these programmes. As Iran's missile programme has taken shape, the issue of missile range has come to the fore, and threats on each side have increased.

And yet the differences between Iran and Israel essentially concern a third party, the Palestinians, and no bilateral or historical disputes or antagonism colour mutual perceptions. Israelis have therefore seen the current Iranian position as a political one, stemming from the nature of the regime in Tehran, rather than from a considered or historically conditioned assessment of national interest. The implication of this is that Tehran's current hostility could be reversed by a political decision, and Israel's strategic concerns thereby alleviated. Iran's political ferment has therefore held out the hope that the threat of conflict might be reduced, if not eliminated, and Israel has thus been especially eager to ascertain whether political reform in Iran would provide an opening for mutual dialogue and lead to a less adversarial relationship.

A background conditioner bearing on any possible rapprochement is the risk for Israel that it could lead to a reduction of the pressures on Iran without subsequent substantive changes in Iran's policies, nor any reduction of the strategic challenge they represent. That could leave Iran in a much stronger position than before. Israel therefore has to consider the risks of an opening yielding only 'atmospheric' changes.

The Iranian–Israeli Relationship

Despite fiery rhetoric, no Iranian leader has suggested that Iran's support for the Palestinians should extend to direct military involvement. Iran claims the right to a say on this 'Muslim issue' but, as the Supreme Leader observed, basically it is too distant to be Iran's *jihad*.[23] This remains an authoritative expression of official policy. President Khatami, despite strong rhetoric, has also noted that Iran considers the question of Palestine a 'major humanitarian issue'.[24] Nevertheless, Iran's support for rejectionists and its development of missiles has led to periodic exchanges of military threats, with Israel threatening to prevent the proliferation of WMD in the region by destroying associated facilities, and Iran threatening retaliation against such an attack.[25]

Iran uses the Israeli threat as the cause and justification for its development of missiles, which it has offered to 'share' with its Arab and Muslim neighbours. (Typically, President Khatami dismissed a question on Iran's missiles by noting that it is Israel's nuclear weapons, not Iran's missiles, that are dangerous to the region.[26]) Meanwhile references to the threat of a resurgent Iraq are rare to non-existent in this context – it is in fact the dominant concern, but publicly acknowledging it would underline Iranian–Arab divisions, whereas focusing on Israel underlines Iranian–Arab solidarity and a common adversary.

For all that, the political utility of justifying Iran's missile programme by reference to the common Israeli threat does not mean that Iranian officials seek conflict. Nonetheless, even without such an intention, developing capabilities, careless rhetoric and exchanges of threats *do* make (accidental) conflict more likely. To take but one example, since there is little serious public debate about Iran's military policies (beyond generalities, posturing and complaints about victimisation), there is a risk that ideological presuppositions will inadvertently drive policy and make for miscalculation. This is especially true in light of the residual nostalgia (like that of former Guards commander Mohsen Reza'i, mentioned in Chapter 2) for the early phase of the revolution, driven by the martyr complex and the brinksmanship implicit in that approach to strategy.

From a domestic political viewpoint, Khatami has little reason to differ from his hard-line opponents on this matter. Given the priority attached to bringing about domestic change (and normalisation with Iran's immediate neighbours), he has little energy or incentive to get involved in other contentious issues. So, putting aside his own feelings (whatever they may be), Khatami has no mandate for a change of policy on this issue, and little reason to seek one – especially given the Supreme Leader's strong personal position on this issue, which is linked both to Iran's revolutionary identity and to its ambitions for a leadership role regionally. Furthermore, Iran's security and its legitimate defence interests, including the development of modern weapons, are not issues that divide reformer and conservative; indeed, tactically, emphasising similarities and common ground between the factions might make it easier for reformers to focus on the key domestic differences. Finally, it serves the reformers' interest to take a strong stance on defence issues and to show themselves just as 'Islamic' as their domestic competitors. Similarly, they have every reason to suggest that, although they are open to the outside world, that does not make them any less nationalistic, and, if in control, they would not prove a 'soft touch' on defence matters. All these considerations have made Iranian reformers less than enthusiastic about seeming to take positions that could be depicted as softer than those of their conservative counterparts. (They have strongly denied reports of informal contacts with Israel, which they see as intended to 'burn' them in terms of domestic politics.)

Israel's approach toward Iran has been on several levels and has not been without its own domestic political conditioners. It has sought to deny weapons-related technology to Iran, to strengthen its own deterrent and improve its defence, and to open a dialogue with Iranian counterparts. The simultaneous pursuit of these policies has created its own tensions. Denying Iran technology has necessitated exaggerating the immediacy and scope of the threat posed by Iran, and emphasising defence and preventive attacks has often been at the cost of undermining deterrence – all of which may make it necessary to engage in dialogue, but doesn't make it any easier to do so.

Israel has reacted to the threat perceived from Iran by exaggerating it for domestic purposes; enhancing deterrence; seeking improved defence, active and passive. Through the US and directly, Israel has also been active in seeking to slow and restrict the transfer of weapons-related technology from Russia, China, Ukraine and other states. The Iranian missile programme has been dependent on these and other sources and has been, and will remain, vulnerable to restrictions.[27] Given Iran's assertion of the right to technology for defence, attempts to restrict technology that has civilian applications (which is true of the underlying technologies in missiles and all WMD: i.e., electronics, biotechnology and chemicals) are seen as hostile acts and attempts to choke Iran's development. Israel's claims of being concerned by Iran's defence programmes – while itself having a monopoly of nuclear weapons and across-the-board superiority in missiles, conventional forces, aircraft, biological and chemical weapons (BW and CW), and at the same time refusing to be bound by international conventions (e.g. the NPT) – find few sympathisers in Iran.

Against this background there were reports of efforts by Israel to establish contact within months of President Khatami's inauguration. Some gestures, such as the return of funds owed to Iran, were made by the Netanyahu government, but reported disappointment with the reaction saw a return to a renewed emphasis on technology denial.[28] In 1998 the beginning of Iran–US overtures led to a reconsideration again in Israel. *Ha'aretz* (21 June) suggested it was time for Israel to send signals to Iran. Israeli officials continued to note how changes in Iran opened up opportunities for Israel. Under the Barak government contacts were again called for. The Justice Minister Yossi Beilin noted that under President Khatami Iran had become 'more nuanced', and that Israel should take its cue from Europe and the US: 'Due to the positive changes evidenced in Iran, there is need to change our approach to them. An opportunity for a new opening is at hand'.[29]

Such overtures were not rewarded. Yet there were areas of common concern that appeared ripe for some dialogue. With Israel's withdrawal from Lebanon, the one area of actual physical friction, in mid-2000 it appeared that both sides might have an interest in a dialogue. Israeli sources certainly hoped for a dialogue to keep the northern border quiet.[30] But this overestimated Iranian restraint. It was hard to resist the temptation to depict the departure of Israeli troops from Lebanon as anything other than victory for Hezbollah. (The implication, of course, was that Hezbollah provided a model for comparable victory in the overall settlement of the Palestinian question.)

The one area where contacts may have taken place is in an informal 'strategic dialogue' in 1999 – though this has been denied by Iran. In June 1999 *Ha'aretz* reported informal contacts between Israel and Iran on defence issues, through the assistance of the United Kingdom. This and later reports suggested that the talks initiated by the Barak government centred on strategic issues, and specifically on suggestions that the two sides renounce (a) the first use of surface-to-surface missiles (SSM); and (b) the intention to arm missiles with WMD warheads. The subject was reportedly raised again on the sidelines of the International Atomic Energy Agency (IAEA) meeting later that year with the Iranians calling for Israel to place its nuclear facilities under full-scope safeguards.[31]

We do not know whether these meetings took place, or what, if anything, was agreed if they did. It is clear that, while Khatami cannot acknowledge such meetings, they would serve a very useful function. Given the pressures on either side, the absence of dialogue makes it harder to establish each party's 'red lines' and makes unintended conflict possible. This is all the more so when the Palestine issue is at boiling point, and temptation to flaunt its support for the new *intifada*, on one side, and frustration at the limited utility of force, on the other, make for more strained relations.[32]

Missiles in Iran's Strategy

Iran sees missiles as its preferred instrument for securing a greater role in international affairs. They are legal (not expressly banned), attainable, and hold out the potential of being equalisers. For Iran, which faces difficulties in acquiring and maintaining a modern air force and has little faith in the reliability of supplies from others, missiles appear to meet the bill: an affordable path to self-reliance and a feasible way of assuring its legitimate defence needs.

Missiles serve three functions in its current foreign and defence policy. First, they act as a deterrent – against Iraq, Israel, the US and any other putative adversary. Second, they serve to symbolise Iran's ascendancy as a regional power, a power to be reckoned with, and taken into account in regional affairs. Third, they serve to act as a counterweight and to offset the United States' military presence in and around the Persian Gulf and potentially in the Caspian Sea.

Iran's immediate strategic environment has been the locus of several serious conflicts, some of which (like those in Afghanistan, Iraq or the Middle East) remain on the boil. In all of these, missiles have been used, and there is a strong probability that they will be again in future. This permissive environment for use has led to a 'missile culture' that appears both pervasive and destabilising;[33] moreover, the United States' frequent resort to missiles of all kinds in the Middle East and elsewhere has underlined for some the need to acquire equivalent weapons to 'dissuade the United States from playing Rambo'.[34] President Khatami has been no less eager than others to emphasise Iran's 'right to science and technology', and missiles (electronics, propulsion, guidance, etc.) are seen as integral parts of modern technology:

> We have decided to be powerful: Powerful in the sphere of armed forces. Powerful in terms of security. Powerful in science, in economy … . Today our armed forces have taken bold steps forward in the scientific and technical spheres … [35]

Iranian officials see defence and related industries as the cutting edge, or driver, for Iran's scientific and technological progress. If no state can develop without modern science, and security today requires an advanced defence infrastructure, it is the task of the government to ensure this by financing and organising it. Hence defence and development are not competitors for resources but are intimately linked, and it is the government's job to ensure their smooth functioning. Thus, denial or restriction of (dual-use) technology by suppliers, ostensibly for security reasons, is in reality a thin pretext for preventing other states' development and maintaining domination over them. This suggests that the more constraints are put on technology in the name of security such as the MTCR, the more Iran will exert itself to achieve the development that it insists it is being denied.

Hostile slogans against the US and Israel, written on the sides of missiles shown in parades or before a test launch, are intended for domestic consumption rather than as serious threats or statements of intent. Such slogans reflect Iran's self-absorption and insensitivity to others' security perceptions, but they also attest to a sense of pride in transcending the overwhelming sense of powerlessness of the past. Missiles thus have powerful symbolic connotations in terms of domestic politics, where a cheer-leading element equates 'advances' with success and progress that bolster the achievements of the Islamic Republic as a whole. Iran's argument that its seeks a missile industry as a step towards developing a space industry in the future may not be universally credited, but does have a superficial plausibility. Technologies today cannot easily be separated, and space launch vehicles are not wholly dissimilar to missiles intended to re-enter the earth's atmosphere aimed at a particular target.

States that seek self-reliance in defence materials usually find the quest expensive and seek to reduce the unit cost of arms produced for home consumption by exporting arms as well. Exports may also have the added bonus of signalling a country's 'arrival' as a power. Iran is no exception to this, and Abu Dhabi's IDEX military fair in 2001 saw a variety of Iran's missiles prominently displayed – they were reported to 'have drawn the attention of all visitors and correspondents'.[36]

Iran's actual *use* of missiles has been rather limited. Despite Taliban threats to use missiles against its cities if Iran entered Afghan territory in the autumn of 1998, Iran resisted making similar threats in response. However, it has repeatedly used missiles to attack *Mujahiddin* (MKOI) bases in Iraq. Almost annually since 1992 these attacks with short-range missiles have followed MKOI attacks on Iranian targets; a recent series occurred in April 2001. It is difficult to resist the conclusion that besides retaliation, these strikes also signal Iran's general military capacity, to Iraq especially but more broadly to the region as well. Iran may also have meant to send a political message through its decision to speed up the testing of its *Shihab*-3 missile, in response to the decisions of India and Pakistan to test their nuclear weapons in mid-1998. [37]

Whatever the effectiveness of missiles as a means of sending messages, it is not clear that the message is always received as intended (or, indeed, that the recipient is always the addressee). Notwithstanding its defensive orientation, Iran's inclination to announce its 'arrival' as a power and to posture domestically does not make it an easy neighbour. Turkey is clearly concerned enough about Iran's nascent WMD capabilities to engage in discussions with the US about sites for a regional TMD system. (Israel may find it useful to remind Turkey of the threat posed by the *Shihab*-3, but Turkey needs little encouragement to monitor its development.) The resulting spectre of Israeli–Turkish military cooperation backed by the US and a complaisant Azerbaijan, in turn feeds Iran's security anxieties about encirclement by a US-led NATO.[38]

The need to defuse the tensions that the growth of new capabilities can accentuate is all too apparent in Iran's relations with Israel and has the potential to become so in relations with Turkey. Insecurity, uncertainty and ambiguity tend to aggravate tensions, and by their nature, missiles tend to be seen as weapons that cannot be easily controlled or fine-tuned in crises. They also make more real the fear of surprise attacks, disarming first strikes and terror attacks aimed at cities. Iranian declarations have been contradictory and have done little to alleviate its neighbours' concerns on these issues.

The development of long-range ballistic missiles (i.e., with ranges greater than needed for immediate and obvious security concerns) raises issues about ultimate objectives. It is true, however, that few states limit their defence capabilities tightly to what they strictly need, and most seek a margin of capability for the unexpected contingency (or for safety or simple advantage). Furthermore, defence needs are rarely simply a matter of rationality, but rather an interaction of what is technologically possible and the interplay of inter-service politics, budgets and military clout. Such interpretations would extenuate or contextualise Iran's missile programme – but Iran's image (and in some respects its past behaviour) do not lend themselves to benign interpretations of its motives. The onus is on Iran to make its missiles appear less threatening to its neighbours. To do this, it will have to speak with one voice and avoid resorting to boasting for (domestic) political effect.

Reformists do not substantially differ from conservatives on Iran's need for an adequate defence capability, nor on its refusal to have its needs defined for it, technologically and morally, by states with their own motives. Nonetheless, the reform faction does not have the same sense of embattlement as their conservative counterpart. For example, after the missile attacks on the MKOI in 2001, one paper proposed a more delicate approach:

> *The main missile which can be used against this [opposition] group can be found in the depot of the country's extensive development, the consolidation of political development will fire the trigger of those missiles.*[39]

Iran will find itself under considerable pressure regionally if US plans to develop a theatre missile defence take shape. Besides Turkey, the GCC states will also be involved in some fashion, and Iran will need to resist the temptation to lash out and to jeopardise the gains it has made in building confidence with them. In the event of a determined US campaign to press for a regional missile defence system, though, reformers in Iran would find themselves under pressure to join the conservatives on the nationalist bandwagon.

Iran sees its missiles as a necessary element of its defence posture. It sees them as instruments of deterrence, primarily (and privately) against Iraq and more publicly as a retaliatory force against Israel. It sees no reason to consider missiles morally more objectionable than any other weapon system, and interprets attempts to constrain its development of them as examples of hypocrisy and selectivity.

To make this case more effectively, Iran could:

- pledge no nuclear or other WMD warheads on missiles;
- pledge a 'no-first-use' doctrine;
- pledge a counter-force targeting policy;
- refrain from the reflexive use of missiles in cross-border attacks against Iraq;
- pursue an informal strategic dialogue with Israel on 'red lines';
- discuss in general terms with GCC states the conditions under which missile ranges and aircraft capabilities could be compared and how/when to include Iraq in discussions.

Dealing with the destabilising regional impact of missile proliferation is very difficult in the absence of agreed international norms. Differential stages of capability, the problems of dual-use technology (peaceful space-launched vehicles are legitimate), and denial policies used selectively complicate any regional agreement, which needs at a minimum some contact between the concerned parties. What appears clear to at least one study is that 'a culture of openness is necessary for future controls on missile activity'.[40] Although Iran's missile capabilities have grown, they should not be exaggerated. They have been dependent on several sources (North Korea, China and, especially, Russia) on which they will continue to depend significantly. There is some time to influence the pace and nature of Iranian missile development, and the greatest chance for influencing this will be through a policy that combines denial with incentives and political engagement.

Chapter 4

Nuclear Weapons

Unlike missiles, which are not banned by any specific international treaty, the possession and development of weapons of mass destruction (nuclear, chemical and biological) are specifically proscribed by the Nuclear Non-Proliferation Treaty (NPT) and the Chemical Weapons and Biological Weapons conventions, to which Iran has solemnly adhered. Iran does therefore not admit to possessing these weapons, and so cannot discuss any doctrine for their use. Consequently its nuclear (and indeed WMD) programmes exist in a penumbra, in which Western (mainly US) allegations of their existence are matched by vehement denials from Tehran, coupled with accusations of selectivity and bad faith by those making the allegations.

Western allegations of clandestine Iranian programmes are based on a cumulative picture derived from patterns of procurement, research activities and monitoring, as well as suspicions of intent based on assumed motivations to possess a WMD weapons capability. The independent analyst cannot refute or confirm these allegations but must make assumptions about the programmes and infer intentions, possible doctrines, etc., from analogous cases and examples. There are also the manifold difficulties of assessing the significance of Iranian statements. Are they authoritative? Are they credited by those making them? Are they intended as excuses and public justifications for programmes being secretly developed? Do the diplomats in fact know what is happening in these programmes?

In this section, which falls into two parts, I start by accepting that Iran might be developing WMD, and discuss its possible reasons for doing so and the variety of constraints operating on it. In the second part, I ask what effect the political competition and emergence of the reformist movement might have on these programmes (I focus on the nuclear programme, but in broad terms the discussion is applicable to CW and BW as well).

Rationales and Constraints

Given the importance that the Islamic Republic of Iran attaches to independence, self-reliance, and equality and respect, it is doubtful that it would have joined the NPT if it had not inherited membership from the regime it overthrew.

Even sympathetic American experts observe that, although the IAEA deems Iran to be in compliance with the NPT, Iran's 'nuclear power program makes no economic sense, and Iran has attempted to purchase equipment vital for nuclear weapons and little else'.[1] Iran's responses to allegations that it is developing a clandestine nuclear weapons programme are not always consistent. They range from blunt denial to the accusation that claims of Iran's non-compliance are intended to divert attention from the most serious case of non-adherence to the NPT: that of Israel. Iranian officials point to their country's membership of all the major arms-control treaties (a record matched only by Jordan in the context of the Middle East); its good standing *vis-à-vis* the IAEA and its inspections of nuclear installations; and its early advocacy of arms-control proposals — e.g. one for a nuclear-weapons-free-zone (NWFZ) in the region, dating to 1974. Iran argues that continuing its nuclear power programme makes sense, given the sunk costs of the Bushire project, which is being revived.

As a member of the NPT, Iran clearly does not (and cannot) seek to justify a quest for nuclear weapons, but must rather insist on its right to develop its nuclear infrastructure unobstructed. Iranian statements on this are clear and Rafsanjani has pointed to the 'unending hostility' of the US.[2] Iran insists on its 'right to technology' to develop its scientific infrastructure 'for peaceful purposes' (a 'right' enshrined in the same conventions that ban weapons production and development) and depicts attempts to interfere with this as discriminatory and hostile. It also plays the victim, pointing to its suffering as a result of Iraq's illegal use of chemical weapons as a reason why it would not develop such weapons. It further observes that US allegations are intended to serve the purpose of justifying that country's controversial national missile defence programme.

Iran usually couples denial of weapons intentions with warnings that the NPT, and controls on the spread of nuclear weapons, cannot be effective if applied selectively, either regionally or globally. In the aftermath of the nuclearisation of the Indian subcontinent, Rafsanjani noted that the international reaction to the Indian nuclear test was disproportionate, given the size of the country and the (rudimentary) level of its nuclear development, compared to tiny Israel and its advanced programme – yet, 'when they talk about nuclear weapons they don't mention the Zionist regime'. Rafsanjani suggested that retaining nuclear weapons as the 'exclusive right' of the existing NWS, together with the toleration of Israel's nuclear capacity, made non-proliferation 'a truly futile expectation' and proliferation 'contagious'. He identified the nuclear tests by India and Pakistan as a seminal event: 'This is major step towards rivalry and proliferation of nuclear weapons. This is truly a dangerous matter and we must be concerned.'[3] Khatami made the same point clearly: Iran opposed 'the proliferation of *all* atomic weapons and *all* weapons of mass destruction' and is prepared to cooperate with others to free the region from them.[4]

These denials of intent to develop weapons and denunciations of Israel's nuclear capabilities and the continued existence of nuclear weapons in the world lack persuasiveness to the Western ear. After all, Iran and Israel have no obvious reasons to fight, and the existence of nuclear weapons was taken as a given by the NPT. Anomalous, too, is the fact that Iranian statements seldom point to the obvious proximate threat to Iran: Iraq. Nor does Iranian policy suggest serious concern about Baghdad – otherwise Tehran would do more to support arms-control monitoring by UNMOVIC, the successor to UNSCOM. Perhaps Iranian officials believe there is greater regional mileage in pointing to the theoretical Israeli threat rather than to the actual threat next door.[5] This may be because justifying any Iranian nuclear weapons by reference to an Iraqi threat would arouse more concerns in the Arab world than attributing them to a 'common' Israeli threat.[6]

That said, what are Iran's motives and what are the constraints on a nuclear weapons programme? Seeking a nuclear weapons option would be consistent with the key principles animating the revolution: self-reliance; independence and equality. More concretely, nuclear weapons might constitute a prudent hedge against the emergence or re-emergence of such weapons in the immediate region – an insurance policy against future strategic surprises. Nuclear weapons might hold attractions for a state lacking dependable access to advanced (expensive) conventional arms and deprived of strategic allies, suppliers and friends. As an equaliser, such weapons would appear to meet Iran's need to be 'taken seriously' and, at a pinch, might substitute for a weak conventional arms infrastructure and provide Iran with an all-purpose diplomatic or military instrument. At this level of analysis, such arguments may appear plausible, though whether Iranian officials think this way, we simply have no way of telling.

At another, more operational level, the problems multiply. First, Iran's programme has been characterised by persistence rather than speed; it is not a crash programme, and it appears to be opportunist rather than carefully mapped out. Still in its infancy, thus dependent on foreign sources of technology and training and so vulnerable to interruption, it will not be self sufficient for the foreseeable future. The programme thus falls into the category of what Brad Roberts has called 'no urgent strategic rationale'. Indeed, Iran has no existential threats or historic enemies, as Pakistan or Israel do. More exact parallels might be with India or China – great civilisations that consider themselves rightfully great powers, and hence entitled to nuclear weapons and the status they are believed to bestow.[7] A regime that seeks influence and a greater say in regional and international affairs might see possessing nuclear weapons as a way to amplify its voice and get the attention of great powers. Nuclear weapons as a bargaining chip, and for leverage, therefore cannot be discounted.

Although some analysts, echoing Iranian officials, have made the case that Iran's 'dangerous neighbourhood' and its need for costly upgrades to its conventional arms provide rationales for nuclear weapons, the fact is that nuclear weapons do not have a clear military rationale for Iran. Its immediate surroundings are indeed turbulent, but there is no obvious way in which nuclear weapons could be relevant in pacifying that environment. From the Taliban and the Afghan wars to the attendant drug wars, from Tajikistan's civil war to Iran's differences with Azerbaijan over the Caspian, and from the Kurdish question to the future of Iraq, none of the disputes or crises would be materially affected by Iran's acquisition of nuclear weapons.

Nuclear weapons may appear to give a pleasing symmetry to Iran's relations with Israel or the US, but the reality would be quite different. Acquiring such weapons would put Iran into a different league of risk and reprisal, and this would not necessarily leave it with enhanced security. Also, the notion that status and nuclear weapons go together may have been weakened by the case of an unstable and indigent Pakistan.

Apart from the limited utility of nuclear weapons in practice and their doubtful justification as a source of status, Iranian efforts to acquire or produce them are inhibited by a number of factors: practical, legal, political and utilitarian. The practical difficulties are dependence on foreign technology and training. Bypassing these by buying (or stealing) fissile material would achieve little, for material thus obtained could produce a handful of weapons (at best), and the problem of longer term self-sufficiency would remain – what state would want to rely on a few weapons that were not renewable? Other practical constraints must revolve around the capacity of the Islamic Republic to produce and retain adequate numbers of scientists and technologists of the calibre to put together an indigenous programme. Given the current brain drain, which includes skilled workers, this may be problematic. And whether Iran has the organisational capacity to run a long-term, integrated, clandestine programme and insulate it from the vagaries of political and personnel changes, from budgetary pressures and from leaks must also be open to question.

Legal constraints are also a consideration. As a signatory of the NPT, Iran has made a solemn commitment renouncing any right to develop nuclear weapons. It is subject to IAEA inspections which, while only sporadic and limited in their effectiveness, still provide a benchmark for compliance. Since Iraq's use of NPT membership to cover its weapons programme, Western intelligence agencies have redoubled their efforts to uncover other clandestine programmes through sustained monitoring of suspect states such as Iran, and, while intelligence may not be adequate to discover the determined and ingenious proliferater, the possibility of discovery must serve as a deterrent to the less-than-strongly-committed proliferater. Other, tighter, controls in future may be difficult to resist: e.g. the enhanced safeguards systems (93 + 2), which still await ratification by many states, including Iran. The risk of discovery may be a deterrent, in that it is unclear what the Security Council would do when faced by a clear violation. Certainly a clear violation (the proverbial smoking gun) would see some reaction on the part of the Security Council, the European Union and Japan, important partners for Iran. This must act as a deterrent to overt violation of the NPT, but may not be enough to stop a programme that seeks to develop something close to a weapons option 'within the treaty'.

Political considerations are more daunting. They revolve around the political costs of being found in violation of the treaty or of withdrawing from the treaty. Withdrawal from the treaty, envisaged in Article X (in the case of 'extraordinary' circumstances threatening 'supreme interests'), has never been attempted, with the partial exception of North Korea. The reaction of other states in the region – Turkey, Saudi Arabia, Israel and Iraq – would have to be considered, including the net effect on Iran's security after their reactions were registered.[8] Violation of the treaty probably would entail severe sanctions and the reversal of the improvement of relations with Europe, the GCC and Japan. However, this is a probability, not a certainty, for Iran might calculate that years of warnings about Iranian nuclear intentions may have dulled these states' concerns, and that simple resignation and economic calculation (Iran remains an important potential market) or pragmatic considerations (it is better to maintain ties with a new nuclear state than to isolate it) may soften any response. A determined state might believe it could get close to a weapons option without discovery, and might convince itself that, in any case, the reaction to its cheating will be minimal.

There are also utilitarian considerations. What are atomic or nuclear weapons for? What *practical* uses do they have beyond deterrence of major (i.e. existential) threats against the homeland? (We have repeatedly seen that they do not deter lesser threats). Iranian leaders seem to equate nuclear power with advanced science and technology skills, though some also note that they divert resources from more pressing social goals.[9] In any case, nobody suggests that nuclear weapons reduce the need for conventional weapons, which are costly, let alone replace them – so the cost of nuclear weapons is in addition to that of conventional ones, which does not make them a cheap or easy all-purpose substitute.

Since Iran denies either possessing or seeking nuclear weapons, there is no authoritative, explicit or focused discussion of how Iran sees nuclear weapons or the type of doctrine it would adopt if it did have them. Nevertheless, it is possible to speculate about this, based on what we do know.

Iranian officials have argued that they never retaliated in kind against Iraq for its use of chemical weapons during the Iran–Iraq war, because of Iran's 'belief in lofty Islamic teachings, and in spite of the silence maintained by most countries and international forums'.[10] Yet the lesson drawn from that war, of preventing future technological and strategic surprises and of relying on one's own resources, would seem to argue for developing any deterrent necessary for future contingencies. And Iran's strategic pragmatism would favour hedging against a repetition of the traumatic effects of chemical weapons use by developing options that could serve as a deterrent and, if necessary, a weapon of retaliation. Taking out such strategic insurance conflicts with Iran's international obligations, so it is logical to infer that one or the other of these must bend a little – hence the steps taken towards developing an option 'within the treaty'. During the war with Iraq, Iran maintained that technology could not substitute for commitment, and willingness to 'give martyrs' guaranteed victory. This argument was not validated by the war's outcome, and is no longer made, and the appetite for martyrdom in Iran has diminished palpably over the past decade.[11]

Iran frequently holds military exercises that include provision for defence against the use of WMD by an adversary.[12] While this could indicate preparations for offensive use by Iran, a more plausible alternative interpretation is that it represents an attempt to prepare and signal defence preparedness to regional states that might be tempted (again) to use WMD in a future conflict. There is no basis for arguing that Iran sees WMD as a means of intimidating its neighbours, or indeed US forces in the Persian Gulf.

It seems unlikely that Iranian leaders have a very developed sense of what nuclear weapons could do, or be used for. Iran Defence Minister Shamkhani, for one, has suggested that US ships in the Persian Gulf may have nuclear weapons aboard, and that the US would use nuclear weapons against Iraq.[13] Neither of these comments suggest any familiarity with the distinguishing characteristics of nuclear weapons, and especially not with the restrictions on their use in most conceivable circumstances (they also confuse depleted uranium shells with nuclear weapons). From their statements, Iranian leaders appear to believe that Israel, despite never having formally acknowledged a nuclear-weapons capability, or made any explicit nuclear threats, is a regional and global threat. This suggests a belief that even an undeclared capability has diplomatic benefits.[14]

This raises a related question: if Iran seeks a nuclear weapons option, where are nuclear-related decisions made? Iran has no military lobby for the 'bomb', like Pakistan, nor a civilian-scientific lobby, like India. If a decision has been made to go towards nuclear weapons under cover of a peaceful programme, it would have been made by a few politicians outside the major co-ordinating agency for decisions affecting national security: the Supreme National Security Council. This is because that Council (whose long-serving Secretary is Hasan Rowhani) has a membership that is not fixed and whose changes reflect political appointments. Given such a turnover, there would not be much assurance of secrecy for the programme. Similarly, the Iranian Head of the Atomic Energy Agency has not remained fixed, changing for example with Khatami's arrival as prime minister in 1977. The most likely 'father of the bomb' in Iran is Rafsanjani, who, despite several changes of job (Speaker of Parliament, President and now President of the Expediency Council), has been in sensitive positions since the beginning of the revolution. Though Rafsanjani holds no formal role in the security area today, he has over the years been the official with the most to say about those programmes related to WMD (and strategy in general), easily displacing Khatami, Khamene'i and others in the number and depth of his statements on these issues.

Given the secrecy, the question of how these weapons are viewed as instruments of diplomacy and war becomes relevant, for despite Iran's relative political openness, issues of national security are still decided more on the opaque North Korean than the Indian model.[15] If there is a small group behind the programme, its members' views of what these weapons' functions are, and what sort of capability Iran should seek, will tend to be insulated from critical scrutiny, debate and above all testing against the historical record. Such a decision-making system would most likely lead to a quest for a general capability – that is, one without a purposive programme or clearly defined and specific ends. It might be opportunist, but it is unlikely to be set in concrete and irreversible, should events warrant it.

If decision-making is indeed limited to a small number of people relatively ignorant of the technical, political and strategic characteristics of nuclear weapons, the question of what is an appropriate Western policy assumes importance. Pressure, sanctions, an embargo on conventional arms, attempts to isolate Iran, on the one hand, and selectivity in concerns about proliferation, on the other, have certainly all given Iranian officials ammunition and psychological incentive to show their adversaries that they will not be dictated to. Marginalising Iran, refusing to consult it where its interests are involved, and generally demonising it will surely strengthen voices in Iran that argue for more international leverage and silence those who might suggest otherwise. And nuclear weapons, at least in the popular or vulgar conception, are still thought to be weapons conferring status and influence.

I have argued that, while Iran may be seeking a nuclear-weapons capability, it has little chance of achieving an indigenous capability in the next decade; it will be reliant on external suppliers for technology and training; in terms of its pressing, relevant security concerns there is little practical utility to acquiring nuclear weapons; and a host of practical, legal and political constraints circumscribe Iran's programme and its utility inside or outside the NPT. The programme seems to be largely the project of a few people, of which Rafsanjani is the most notable, and it appears open-ended and not purposive in the sense of having specific ends or a timetable. Western policies may have contributed to the decision to start and continue down this road. The pace, and even the evolution of the programme itself, which is not irreversible, will depend on the political atmosphere and environment as much as on technical or financial considerations. Improved relations with the US would certainly reduce the rationale and justification for it, which may explain the resistance of the conservatives in Tehran to any improvement in such relations.

Politics and the Nuclear Weapons 'Debate' in Iran

In the argument that Iran is implacably opposed to WMD, public opinion is invoked by Iranians, sometimes as a constraint and at other times as a source of pressure likely to question why, given its hostile neighbourhood, Iran denies itself certain arms. But does public opinion as such exist? The politicisation of the populace and the Khatami phenomenon, together, do suggest much more than a compliant or inert mass. However priorities are domestic, focused on the bread-and-butter issues of the day. Where WMD are concerned, public debate seldom gets beyond the broadest generalities, and even expert discussion is seldom sophisticated – and this is especially true of nuclear weapons. So can we talk of a 'debate about nuclear weapons'? Perhaps an indirect, elite debate, which both reflects and forges a national consensus, is more accurate.

Regime politics in every domain involve creating consensus; coalitions vary according to the issues, and these cross-cutting alignments make analysing Iranian politics (and even the reform movement) an intricate and arcane exercise. Furthermore, in practice power tends to be informal as well as formal. Decisions reached can thus be the product of complex tradeoffs and agreements among groups, rather than the outcome of simple, linear, rational processes. None of this suggests that specific defence decisions are made openly.[16] When Iran experienced difficulties with Russia over the agreement to refurbish the Bushire reactor, a newspaper, *Salaam*, ridiculed the project as a joke, and urged the authorities to break their silence and inform the public of the obstacles involved in the project.[17]

Certainly the opportunity costs of defence expenditures (and especially the nuclear component) have risen with the urgency of the need for domestic investment. At the same time, Khatami reflects a more consultative and accountable form of government based on transparency. These factors in combination have increased the inclination (notably by the reformist press) to demand a more open system of decision-making.

Some Iranian officials have argued that not only is forging a consensus for national security 'complicated and time-consuming' – involving the SNSC, *Majlis*, leadership, and academic and governmental experts – but that, once reached, the consensus is subject to the 'careful scrutiny of an ever demanding civil society, the press, political tendencies and groupings, universities, a growing number of NGOs and the general public'. To build a consensus, the authors argue, clear arguments have to be presented, and this in turn necessitates transparency and 'tolerance for a diversity of views'. The implication is that the hard-line view, sometimes selectively quoted by Western analysts, does not tell the whole story and represents just one of a variety of inputs into the decision-making process. For these authors, President Khatami's general platform of seeking détente and normalisation in foreign policy for security, and security for development, has been enthusiastically endorsed by the electorate and so is 'another determinant of Iran's national security formation'.[18]

An incident with Rahim-Safavi in 1998 is indicative. Shortly after a conciliatory CNN interview by Khatami the Guards Commander's remarks to a closed meeting of his officers were leaked by the press. He was quoted as asking:

> *Can we withstand America's threats and domineering attitude with a policy of détente? Can we foil the dangers coming from America through a dialogue of civilisations? Will we be able to protect the Islamic republic from international Zionism by signing conventions banning the proliferation of chemical and nuclear weapons?*[19]

It seems that this questioning, put to a private meeting and not intended for public disclosure, indicates a degree of dissatisfaction with the policy favouring arms control adopted by both Khatami and his predecessor Rafsanjani. It suggests that differences (and possibly debates) exist and take place, albeit within the narrow elite of senior officials.

Public debate is another matter. It appears that there is a debate of sorts about nuclear weapons – or, rather, about *whether* Iran ought to seek a nuclear option. On this, several observations can be made:

- Possibly reflecting differences among the leadership, the public debate is really more about different foreign-policy orientations than technical questions.[20]
- The debate is not polarised between conservatives and reformists, for, as in foreign policy, there is considerable fluidity: some conservatives oppose the development of a nuclear option as of doubtful strategic utility.[21]
- The debate reflects realist or idealist views of the world, and this cuts across ideological alignments. Realists come from both sides of the political spectrum, and some argue for the development of a nuclear option as a 'bargaining chip'.[22] Proponents of an 'option' seek prestige, power and leverage; opponents see such a course as eroding Iran's security, cite Iran's international obligations and seek to enhance security through arms control (a regional nuclear-free zone) and an improved climate in international affairs generally.

Though not terribly well-informed, this debate serves to deepen the involvement of the public in issues of national interest and to lay out in broad terms the general issues concerning a decision to develop a nuclear option.[23] Despite the changed political atmosphere and the stirrings of civil society in Iran sketched out above, it is premature to argue that national security is either transparent or open to public pressures, especially where decisions and policies are made in secret or not announced. If Iran has already decided to develop a clandestine nuclear weapons programme (as the US alleges), this is unlikely to be widely debated even within the national-security apparatus. It can be justified under the broad rubric of 'right to technology' and by emotive reference to the West's double standards *vis-à-vis* Israel, recognising that Iran's actual programme will be hidden from most Iranian officials (e.g. those in the foreign office). In parallel, Iran's diplomatic strategies with respect to arms-control agreements in the nuclear, chemical and biological weapons areas have been to tie its future adherence and support to improved access to technology that is inherently dual-use or ambiguous.

If Iranian officials are exploiting the ambiguities of a right to 'peaceful technologies', and acting the outraged-member-state-in-good-standing-suffering-discrimination, how far is this a national policy – i.e., a deliberate deception to which the reformists, including President Khatami, are privy? Most analysts believe that political competition in Iran is genuine and would preclude this degree of dissimulation or 'conspiratorial cover-up'.[24]

How does political competition (and, more precisely, the reformist movement) affect decisions in this sensitive area of national security if denied information about it and not in control of the agencies of government that run the programmes? As national interest has become the touchstone of Iran's foreign and security policies, so the desire realistically to match Iran's needs and capabilities has also gained ground. No longer embattled, Iran has sought to diminish its isolation by forswearing indiscriminate hostility and the promotion of values with little direct relevance to its national needs. Along with fence-mending and rebuilding international contacts has come recognition of the need for Iran to reinvigorate its domestic economy. Despite the primacy accorded to domestic politics, genuine reform has been stymied by the conservatives, and economic reform lags even further behind. However, the pressures for an accountable and responsive government, and the trend towards validating the regime by performance legitimacy (rather than divinely ordained sanction), means that Iranian officials will have to consider their expenditures and their policies more carefully, lest they be publicly revealed. Policies are now subject to ventilation and, if leaked, to scrutiny and criticism.

We may summarise the impact of the reformists thus. Insofar as they reflect and stimulate a more open society with debate and accountability, they increase pressures for transparency. And, although public opinion may not yet exist as far as highly sensitive and covert programmes are concerned, long-term secrecy may not be possible, and elite opinion (criticism and debate) may influence programmes already adopted.

The reformists are no more monolithic in this area than in other areas, but most would tend to share with the conservatives a sense of patriotism and insistence on the right to self-defence, independence, self-reliance and equality, as well as a desire to play an important international role. Where they differ from the conservatives is in their view of foreign policy generally, specifically with reference to the value of détente, dialogue and cooperative security. Lacking a sense of mission, and having a different conception of what Iran represents (a democratic republic as well as an Islamic one) the reformists see interdependence and engagement as desirable (and inevitable). Given the opportunity, they would emphasise arms control as complementary to deterrence and defence.

Such an opportunity may come if they continue their string of election successes, and are able to make inroads into the national security apparatus. As long as the conservatives do not see the nuclear programme as indispensable for regime security (and the evidence is unclear here), it is a project that may be forgone or redefined. Whether reformists' electoral success will lead to eventual influence, or even control, in the sensitive national security institutions, also depends on first, how far the conservatives feel the need to cooperate with the reformists to maintain the regime; and second, how far the reformists can 'deliver' the social peace that is the price for the hard-liners tolerating them.

If, as argued, the nuclear weapons programme is not irreversible, and has a considerable way to run, the reformists' changing of the foreign policy environment could highlight both the costs and the practical limitations on the utility of nuclear weapons.[25] This might make it easier for Iran to consider practical measures to enhance its access to technology and improve its security in exchange for greater transparency in its nuclear programmes. A start might be to accept the enhanced 93 + 2 safeguards system already on the table, in exchange for better access to technology; accepting

Iran's legitimate defence needs instead of applying blanket restrictions on arms transfers from the West might be a complementary step. None of this is likely to happen until both Iran and the West come to favour such an approach and start a dialogue as a result.

To conclude this section, I have argued that there are plausible political reasons for Iran to reject on principle the notion of inequality (inherent in the NPT) and seek a nuclear-weapons capability. There are, however, a host of problems associated with seeking a nuclear-weapons option: political, legal, financial as well as practical. The last category include manpower and organisational deficiencies which will work against a successful clandestine domestic programme. A weapons programme that depends on importing fissile material and on foreign specialists has inbuilt limitations, and so can scarcely be characterised as self-reliant or depicted as a signal triumph, adding lustre to the regime's status; moreover such a programme would provide little assurance from a defence and security standpoint. Iran's indigenous means and access to fissile material are limited and will necessarily take a considerable time to develop, and achieving self-sufficiency will be problematic, even with foreign expert assistance. There are also constraints on the effective use of nuclear ambiguity within the NPT (these apply to Iran, which is a signatory, but not to Israel, which is not) and serious penalties to consider if withdrawal is contemplated. Furthermore Iran's political situation is in a state of flux: a situation that is not conducive to the pursuit of a programme requiring significant resources and secrecy over a long time. This is not to suggest that Iran has no incentives to develop nuclear technology that takes it close to nuclear weapons. But the movement from civilian uses to weaponisation is not inevitable – and has perhaps been arrested by the arrival of the reformists in Iranian politics. Whether it can be reversed depends on the broader security environment and on how politics within Iran evolve in future.

Chapter 5

Terrorism and the Middle East Question

Terrorism is the tactic most associated with the Islamic Republic of Iran. Its use of terrorism as an instrument of coercion and intimidation was widespread, even routine, during its first decade and a half of existence. The result was to increase Iran's isolation, confirm its status as a pariah state and reinforce its sense of embattlement. More recently, partly as a result of changes in its politics (and society), Iran has substantially repudiated this tactic, which has been morally discredited. For Iran today, terrorism is confined to the assistance extended to Palestinian groupings in support of their 'liberation struggle'. This is closely tied to Iran's policy on the Arab–Israeli issue, which, in turn, is tied to Iran's continued attempts to adopt a posture of leadership in the Islamic world. This posture has practical benefits for Iran, but it also has other – symbolic – connotations, reflecting Iran's continuing revolutionary mission. Just as domestic political pressures have dramatically circumscribed Iran's reliance on terrorism, the stirrings of debate on an appropriate Middle East policy will, in time, similarly affect its opportunistic exploitation of the Palestine issue.

The Islamic Republic of Iran has been associated with terrorism from its inception and has figured on lists of terrorist states or state sponsors of terrorism annually.[1] Given the breadth of the accusations from a variety of sources that it was involved in some capacity in terrorist acts from North Africa to Europe, and from the East Asia to the Middle East, there are few grounds for suspecting their essential veracity. Our concern in the first section of this chapter (before looking at the related question of policy on the Middle East) is to look at Iran's use of terrorism as an instrument of state policy for strategic purposes, and, in the light of a discernible and significant change in policy since Khatami became President to ask what this narrowing use of terrorism can be attributed to. To do this, we need to look briefly at the pre-1997 background, so that we can ask what has changed in the later period.

Iran and the Strategic Use of Terror

Until the mid-1990s, the Islamic Republic was regarded as the leading proponent of a form of warfare that disregarded rules and used fear for political purposes, whether labelled 'state-sponsored terrorism' or (following Tom Schelling) 'violent diplomacy'. In 1993 President Mubarak, asked whether he had a message for Iran, replied: 'Stop terrorism'.[2] After bombings of Jewish targets in Buenos Aires and London in 1994, Prime Minister Yitzhak Rabin echoed this, stating that 'the world must wake up to the acute danger posed by Islamic movements, some of which are linked to Iranian elements'.[3] Rabin told the *Knesset* that these attacks were intended to harm the peace process:

> *The radical Islamic terrorist organizations are trying to harm moderate Arab regimes prepared for peace with Israel. In recent years, Iranian aid to such terrorism both direct and indirect, has been prominent. Iran's involvement is found in the attacks carried out by the radical Islamic elements in the Middle East and around the world. ....we shall fight against Khomeynism without Khomeyni, which is the main axis characterizing the wave of radical Islamic terrorism.[4]*

Jordanian and Palestinian officials claimed that Iran was financing 'fundamentalists' and training extremist groups hostile to the peace process.[5] The Palestinian Authority's inability to reach agreement with Hamas and Islamic Jihad to cease terrorist attacks in and around the areas under Palestinian control, Rabin attributed to external interference, specifically from Iran. Shimon Peres went further, saying that Iran supported Hezbollah, Islamic Jihad and Hamas and transferred war materiel, training equipment and funds to them. He noted that not a single word uttered by Iranians could be trusted.[6]

Allegations of Iranian terrorism have not been confined to the Arab–Israeli area; in the Persian Gulf Iran has targeted Saudi Arabia and Kuwait in the 1980s and Bahrain in the 1990s. In 1996 an Arab summit conference in Cairo denounced all intervention and called on Iran 'to respect Bahrain's sovereignty ... by preventing any acts of sabotage against the State of Bahrain'.[7]

Iranian denials, for the most part perfunctory, were limited to emphasising three themes:

i. Bias in the West's use of the label of terrorism, which left no room for (legitimate) national resistance and liberation struggle;
ii. Iran's principled opposition to the peace process, which was unfair and a 'sell-out' of Arab interests. (Anti-terrorist conferences, such as that at Sharm al-Shaykh in 1996, use the phrase 'confrontation with terrorism' to mean opposition to those who refuse to accept the peace process).
iii. Iran's status as a victim of terrorism, notably at the hands of the Mujahiddin-e (MKOI).

During this period (1979–1996), Iran's use of terrorism for political ends was fairly extensive, and as much a matter of principle as a pursuit of considered political goals. In this militant phase, Iran sought to expand the revolution and its influence with resources that did not match its ambitions. Terrorism was easily accepted and even congenial to revolutionaries; at a time when the regime was still not consolidated, terrorism was an extension of revolutionary politics: clandestine, coercive and non-attributable. It provided a state with the means to avoid the two extremes of, on the one hand, direct involvement (which might entail confrontation) and, on the other, total abstention (with a diminution in influence). At this time terrorism was not an exceptional tool of state policy; it was a preferred instrument and was used to achieve several political ends. As part of war, it was employed to change policies or eject foes from the region (examples in the 1980s include the US Marine barracks bombings, the bombing of French targets in Lebanon and bombing incidents in Kuwait). It was used for intimidating or subverting neighbours into changing policy (e.g. the

GCC's support for Iraq) to fall into line with Iranian preferences. It served to promote the Iranian 'Islamic' model – for example in Lebanon (and, to a lesser extent, in North Africa and Asia) – and it provided a means of gaining leverage or influence on an issue (most notably on Palestine and the peace process). Domestically, terrorism helped to keep the revolution militant (its use was often an outgrowth of domestic and factional politics), and could be an instrument of regime maintenance and control (e.g. the murder of Iranian opponents abroad and, after 1997, of domestic critics and intellectuals).

During the revolution, and since, the monolithic image often associated with Iranian politics has been contradicted by a decentralisation of power and a related factionalism. Rafsanjani's tenure as President (1989–1997) was just as racked by divisions as Khatami's today (though then they were more intra-elite rivalries than national and popular divisions). Terrorism could be, and was, used by factions to advance their domestic standing as much as for pursuing strategic goals.

Those affected by Iran's terrorism were aware of these divisions. The US, it will be recalled, sought to find 'moderates' in Iran in the Irangate saga in 1986; that episode, leaked by one faction in Iran, was used to settle domestic scores. In 1993, President Mubarak observed: 'We know there are several trends in Iran. There are moderates and the extremists. But ...'.[8] The Palestinian authorities were also aware of domestic differences: 'certain powers in Iran [are] bent on meddling in Palestinian affairs and creating a climate conducive to crime and terror, as they did elsewhere. Certain power centres in Iran are advancing, as a cloak, the pretext of liberating Palestine on religious grounds [when in fact they are] exporting their self-styled Islamic revolution'.[9]

On these issues Iranian politics has been divided, mainly between the extreme and somewhat less extreme. At a time when government officials were pragmatically coming to terms with the fact that Syria might negotiate an agreement with Israel in the context of the peace process in 1995/96, a conservative newspaper noted that in 'abjectly seeking peace' Hafez al Asad was courting the same fate as Anwar Sadat (i.e. assassination) and, for good measure, referred to a recent terrorist bombing in Riyadh, Saudi

Arabia, as indicative of 'what dependence on foreigners brings'.[10] When the US military installation at Al Khobar in Saudi Arabia was bombed in June 1996, Iranian involvement was immediately suspected, but no solid, direct, link has been incontrovertibly established. (Rafsanjani is reported to have indicated to Saudi officials that he, in any case, had been opposed to Iran's involvement,[11] and this is consistent with his veiled warning as he left the Presidency.[12])

Despite differences within the leadership, the use of terrorism as a general policy instrument persisted until 1996. Thereafter it was used much more selectively. Although the turning point coincided with Khatami's election, the change was not exclusively attributable to him, because the combination of a number of factors led Iran to reduce its reliance on terrorism as an instrument of national policy:

- It had proved counterproductive, for Iran found itself practically friendless in the region and beyond, shunned as a threat and a nuisance. Further, Iranian public opinion had turned against this kind of militant, lone-wolf approach to international relations, as Khatami's election on a platform of establishing normal relations with other states reflected. (Khatami's early efforts to deal with the Rushdie case, noted earlier, involved trying to educate his domestic opponents to the proposition that every act entailed a cost.[13])
- In early April 1997, after a German court named Iranian officials (including Intelligence Minister Fallahian) as directly responsible for killings of Iranian Kurds in the Mykonos Restaurant in Berlin, it became clear that the continued use of terrorism with anonymity was becoming more difficult. And the Al Khobar incident provided a reminder of how Iran had courted, and come close to, being identified and targeted militarily.
- A series of murders of domestic political critics of the regime were carried out from 1998 by so-called 'rogue agents' of the Intelligence services, with the apparent approval of senior officials of the regime. This brought home to Iranians how reliance on such means distorted the aims of the revolution, and how the dangers of terrorism were now being turned inwards. In

this climate of revelation and condemnation by the press and public, Iran's practice of international terrorism took on a new perspective.

- Iran was increasingly the object of continuing cross-border terrorism by the MKOI. It had warned Iraq that it would be held responsible for playing host to this group, and periodic military retaliation would be justified accordingly.
- A final impulse flowed from the advent of the fundamentalist Sunni Taliban regime in Afghanistan in 1996. Apart from the normal Sunni–Shi'i antagonisms and Taliban mistreatment of Afghan Shi'i who looked to Iran for support, there was the murder of ten Iranian officials in Mazar-i-Sharif in 1998. With such behaviour making Iran look like a responsible state in comparison, Iran took the opportunity to distance itself from the Afghan regime, condemning its behaviour and, at the same time, registering its opposition to the terrorist blasts in East Africa.

A Touch of Restraint

After 1997/8, therefore, Iran began to distance itself from terrorism, though without renouncing it completely. Since then it has resorted to terrorism only[14] in the context of the Middle East conflict – which it describes as one of national liberation and resistance, rather than terrorism (a view that is not uniquely Iranian). Khatami capped his policy of improving relations with Iran's Gulf neighbours in April 2001 by concluding a 'security agreement' with Saudi Arabia that envisages cooperation in combating terrorism, drug-trafficking and organised crime. This agreement (which took two years to negotiate, thanks to Iranian internal differences) showed that Iran now saw terrorism as a mutual concern shared with its neighbours: a demonstration of how far it had come.

While running for re-election later that year, President Khatami made one of his few references to foreign affairs in a comment on the Rushdie affair: 'We explicitly announce that we are against terrorism in all it shapes, as demanded by our religious, moral and cultural mores, and will seriously fight against this phenomenon'.[15]

Despite these apparent changes, the US still accused Iran of being, as of 2000, the 'most active state sponsor of terrorism'.[16] Its basic allegation is that Iran has become more, rather than less, active in seeking to sabotage the Middle East peace process. Generally, Iran is accused of coordinating, financing and encouraging Hamas, Islamic Jihad and Hezbollah to continue their terrorism against negotiations; it is additionally accused of arming and sometimes of directing Hezbollah's actions. The weight of the evidence from US, Palestinian and Israeli sources, as well Iran's public announcements denying Israel's right to exist and asserting Iran's duty to assist Muslims in their liberation struggle, suggests that Iran has been actively engaged in activities that invite the label 'terrorist' from at least the affected parties. There is no doubt that Iran has rallied the rejectionist forces, held conferences in Iran encouraging them, and given them financial assistance and possibly safe havens. Whether it armed or trained them or has been successful in influencing Islamic Jihad or Hamas directly, is less certain. Nonetheless, the fact is that Iran has not ended its support for those elements that reject the Middle East peace process and has been implicated in acts which many have reason to call terrorist.

The relationship with Hezbollah is a special case in a number of ways. As the only Shi'i state, Iran has considered it its duty to be supportive of Shi'i populations in neighbouring countries, and especially where the Shi'i constitute a majority of the population (Iraq) or a plurality (Lebanon) that, although not actually physically oppressed, lacks proportional political weight. In this respect Iran has had, at best, limited success in Iraq and Afghanistan. However, its links with the Lebanese Shi'i through Hezbollah can be counted a relative success: Hezbollah is now a national force, with eleven parliamentary deputies, and its military tactics (with Iranian training, intelligence, arms and financing) forced Israel to end its occupation of southern Lebanon in mid-2000. [17] Hezbollah constitutes a validation of Iran's model; as Sheikh Hassan Nasrallah put it, what is going on in Iran 'presents a model and an example ... There are a lot of models. Some of them are very dangerous like the Taliban.'[18] And it is not just a civic model but an example of successful resistance, living testimony to the centrality of piety and commitment in the struggle against the Israeli juggernaut. As the Supreme Leader noted:

> *There was no model for resistance in those days [1991]. It*
> *was also believed that such a model would not meet public*
> *acceptance. However we have a successful model in front of*
> *us today, which, for the first time, has been able to free the*
> *occupied lands without making concessions to Israel and has*
> *stopped the Zionist enemy from realising its dream of*
> *planting its flag in the capital of this Arabic country.*[19]

There are a number of explanations for Iran's continuing use of terrorism, and they are mutually reinforcing rather than mutually exclusive (which makes for policies that are incoherent and hard to interpret). One sees it as an instrument in the service of a policy on which there is substantial consensus within the leadership. As discussed in the next section, the country's support for the 'just' Palestinian cause and its taking of a leadership role on a 'Muslim' issue are not yet seriously debated or contested. In this political context the clandestine use of force is seen as a legitimate instrument in the liberation of Arab/Muslim lands. It is also seen as a necessary instrument, playing to Iran's comparative advantage, for Iran, lacking diplomatic standing or other means of influence, would otherwise have little to contribute to the dispute.

Another interpretation sees the use of terrorism as the outgrowth of factional politics: hostility toward the US and Israel are ineluctably tied to the interests of hard-liners, who wish to keep their constituency mobilised and their domestic failures overlooked, and who derive their legitimacy from the sense of mission and embattlement that they foster. Foreign governments are aware of this. In 1999, as a test, the US sought Khatami's help in its inquiry into Al Khobar; this initiative – intended to separate the moderates from the hardliners within Iran – backfired when Khatami used the US overture, which was combined with a threat, to show that he could stand up to US 'bullying' just as well as his political adversaries.[20] Palestinian sources also have assumed factional differences, attributing Iran's 'spoiler' tactics as intended to serve factional ends in the domestic power struggle (for Iran's policy appears to be intended to sabotage any settlement, rather than promote any conceivably realistic alternative settlement).

A third explanation focuses on the role of interest groups, institutional interests or personal ties. I have argued that some areas of national security policy are effectively insulated from debate or scrutiny, even within the leadership. Something similar happens with Iranian military/intelligence assistance in the Lebanese and Palestinian contexts. Here, the main institutions are the Revolutionary Guard and the Ministry of Intelligence and Security, and the President has little involvement.[21] Iranian clerics have long-standing ties and affiliations with Lebanon that transcend political issues, and this may account for the resilience and durability of the connections established. On the political side such individuals as Hojjatoleslam Ali Akbar Motashemipour and Hossein Sheikoleslam, Ambassador to Syria, have dealt with these issues, in one capacity or another, since the beginning of the Islamic Republic.[22] Continuity in the individuals responsible, together with a degree of institutional autonomy and an interest in widening its areas of responsibility and activism, ensure that policies persist, despite political change, and do so without scrutiny or debate.

A fourth interpretation looks to inertia, standard operating procedure and the absence of strong shock necessitating change. One subset of this focuses on the low-cost/high-returns aspect of terrorism: never having had to pay a high price in terms of military retaliation for terrorist ventures (e.g. the Lebanon Marine barracks and Al Khobar bombings, etc.), Iranian officials have not discarded this weapon as ineffective or dangerous. A related subset focuses on culture or operating style. This argues that terrorism is an extension of revolutionary politics: a technique developed in opposition, that, now that the opposition has taken power, is still congenial – a preferred policy tool, secretive and deniable. This fits with other aspects of the style of a regime whose behaviour is characterised by opportunism as much as ideology.

In recent years there has been little dispute among Western powers about the fact of Iranian support for terrorism. The differences have lain in views of what response was appropriate – with the US seeking to isolate and sanction Iran, and the European states seeking to engage it in trade and a 'critical dialogue'. These differences narrowed with the election of Khatami and his attempt to reduce the 'wall of mistrust' through a 'dialogue of civilisations'. Nevertheless, Iran's continued support of rejectionist forces in 2000/2001, and the incidence of terrorist attacks in the second *intifadah* were a source of considerable anger and consternation in the US. The issue of Iran's terrorism was thrown into sharp relief after 11 September 2001 and the catastrophic terrorist attacks by a non-state group, al-Qaeda, on the US.

11 September 2001 and the 'War on Terrorism'

The events of 11 September caused the US to focus as never before on the issue of terrorism as a national security priority. It declared war on international terrorism and vowed to continue that war for as long as was required; its first stage was the destruction of the al-Qaeda network and the sanctuary provided for it by the Taliban in Afghanistan.

In seeking a broadly based international coalition for a long-term, multi-dimensional war on terrorism, the US had to consider Iran's role. On the one hand, as a neighbour to Afghanistan (with which it had bad relations[23]), Iran had the potential to assist the coalition in practical terms; on the other, it was still on the terrorist list, and might be considered a potential target at some stage.

Iran's interests were several. One was the probability that the crisis would see even more refugees entering Iran from Afghanistan, swelling the two million already there. Another direct concern was the apparent legitimisation of the US use of force in the region, with the Afghanistan campaign to the east starting while military operations in Iraq to the west were still not terminated: a prolonged war and a large US military commitment might mean a long stay in the region by US forces. A third consideration was the plight of the hapless, malnourished population of Afghanistan, caught in the middle of military retaliation or a prolonged campaign. Finally, Iran was concerned by the fact that the US could define 'terrorism' to suit its own political agenda and then expect unquestioning support from the international community. This was especially worrying, since initially it was unclear where the war on terrorism (with a global reach) might end up. The possibility that it might affect Iran directly soon emerged when the US published a list of terrorists that it sought, some of whom, allegedly, lived in Iran.[24] Another consideration was that this list might include organisations of what Iran considered freedom fighters, like Hezbollah or Hamas. Out of deference to the Arab world, the US initially left these organisations out of the original list, but within weeks it tightened the sanctions against them.[25] Iran sought to limit US freedom of manoeuvre by calling for a meeting of the Islamic Conference Organisation; when it met in October it condemned the September act of terrorism, but also called for a settlement of the Palestinian question.[26]

All factions in Iran recognised the broad outlines of Iran's interests sketched above, but they differed over how to exploit the opportunity the crisis presented in order to reposition Iran internationally through its regional diplomacy. For the 'reformists' the crisis offered Iran the chance to dissociate itself from its previous practices and turn over a new leaf. Above all, it was an opportunity to act assertively diplomatically – to stake out Iran's interests (in contrast to its passivity in the 1990/91 crisis when its reactiveness had left it empty-handed). The crisis offered Iran an opportunity to use its overlapping interests with the US to start the long delayed dialogue. Against this, the view of the 'conservatives' was that the US was not to be trusted: that it was bombing innocent Muslims, had a strategy of expansion into Central Asia, supported Zionist aggression, defined terrorism selectively, and sought to use the crisis to undermine revolutionary Iran. Their prescription was clear: Iran should resist, and even oppose, the US campaign in Afghanistan.

In sounding out the Iranian leadership, the US and the European states made an asset of their different approaches; in a division of labour, the European states in the shape of Jack Straw, Britain's Foreign Secretary, and a senior EU delegation visited Tehran for consultations. The Iranian response was ambiguous, condemning the attack and terrorism in general, but insisting that the US should use the UN in any response, and expressing doubts as to whether the US alone should be allowed to define terrorism. Iran refused the use of its air space to the coalition and rejected President Bush's idea that there were only two choices: to be on the side of the US or to be with the terrorists. The Supreme Leader said he was opposed to both.

Ayatollah Khamene'i effectively prevented exploitation of the crisis by the reformists, who clearly hoped to use it to strengthen links with the West and improve Iran's overall image.[27] His intervention and his unwillingness to envisage formal or public cooperation with the US, even when interests converged, stopped moves that might have led to a process of reconciliation. The Supreme Leader was explicit: 'not only the relationship with America but also negotiation with that country is against our national interest'.[28]

This did not preclude quiet cooperation, possibly including intelligence-sharing. Iran's support for the Northern Alliance, its flexibility on acceptance of King Zahir Shah as an interim figurehead, were in line with the position of the US. Iran allowed the use of its air space (for rescue missions only), and promised to assist US servicemen in distress on Iranian territory. In addition to intensive contacts with European states[29] and the UN representative, Iran has also had contacts with the US through the existing UN-sponsored 6 + 2 mechanism (i.e. the neighbouring states, plus the US and Russia) and has resumed contact with Pakistan. Given its substantial interest in the replacement of the Taliban, Iran's attitude to the US can be boiled down to: 'do the job quickly and then leave the region'.[30]

The country's reaction to the 11 September crisis and its repercussions reflects a great deal of contemporary Iran: a broad agreement on Iran's interests; an impulse to be active regionally; and a pragmatic attitude towards informal co-operation with the US and the West, combined with an unwillingness to publicise this. Iran's reaction demonstrates the continuing domestic political competition, which looks at each event in foreign policy in terms of its impact on the factions' fortunes domestically.

Iran and the Middle East Question

Iran under Khatami has reduced its support for terrorism as an instrument of policy, but not abandoned (or renounced) it where it considers it a means of support for a liberation movement. The Middle East conflict is not an issue that divides the leadership (although it has not been dispassionately debated either); the outcome of the current wave of international attention and resources devoted to anti-terrorism will, in large part, determine the policies of states associated with it in the future. Whether Iran continues to support the groupings forcibly opposing the peace process, given the priority attention now accorded to the issue of terrorism by major powers, is uncertain. What is clear is that, since 11 September 2001, the price Iran will have to pay for this has risen considerably.

Even under the Shah, the sympathy of most Iranians was probably with their co-religionists, the Palestinians. What was new with the Islamic Republic of Iran was the definition of the dispute as Islamic, and the adoption of positions more hard-line and intractable even than those of the parties concerned: the Palestinians and front-line Arab governments. This entailed taking positions on politico-military issues and elevating the question into one of strategic rivalry with Israel, with the consequences that entailed: aggravated relations with the US and the risk of unintended military conflict.

In this section I discuss Iran's formal position on the Palestine question and assess possible reasons why Iran attributes importance to the issue, including the political uses of adopting this stance. I then ask whether there are significant differences between reformists and conservatives on this issue. Finally I ask what the implications of the current stance are for national security and what might change it.

Palestine: Iran's Policy

Iran's policy has never had a single authoritative expression and tends to take on different colouration depending on the audience being addressed. However, its gist is clear: non-recognition of Israel and support for the Palestinian cause and the right of its people to reclaim occupied lands as their homeland. This implies the destruction or elimination of Israel as the only realistic goal. Iran therefore asks all Muslim states to cut off all relations with Israel, calls for a total trade embargo with that state and its expulsion from the United Nations. Iran sees the Madrid Peace Process as inherently flawed and inevitably unjust, given the prominent US role and Israel's military superiority. Hence Iran supports the Palestinians' resistance – often at the expense of the

Palestine National Authority – and (especially since 2000) the second *intifadah*, not least because it reflects the Iranian-sponsored 'Hezbollah model'. Iran calls support for the Palestine cause 'a Moslem duty' (i.e., not a discretionary issue for governments).

Iran's position has four core points:

i. the right of the Palestinians to their own homeland with Jerusalem as its capital;
ii. the return of occupied territories;
iii. the right of return to Palestine for *all* refugees; and
iv. a referendum on the future of the state once the first three conditions have been satisfied.

Iranian officials insist on the *moral* basis of their policy; that the Palestine issue is the principal issue facing Moslems, and Iran is duty bound to assist. However, the nature of that assistance and its scope and limits is seldom clearly delineated. The Supreme Leader has said that the duty does not extend to direct military involvement:

> *Unfortunately, we cannot take part among the ranks of battle and struggle against an aggressive enemy, because we are far away. We are not duty-bound according to Islamic commands, to go to distant frontiers to take part in fighting and jihad. However, if we were close, it would be our duty to take part in the defence [against the aggressor]. In this case, we cannot.*[31]

Rafsanjani has contrasted Iran's policy in Lebanon with that regarding Palestine:

> *First, no one has proved that we are helping people who are engaged in a holy war inside Israel, as it is within their rights to do. It is clear, and we admit it, that we are involved in southern Lebanon. But as to other areas, we are in no way involved whatsoever. We accept and defend their right to fight but this matter has nothing to do with us. They are defending their rights.*[32]

Iran's determination to take such a stance on an issue which does not directly affect its national security appears quixotic. One explanation might be the obvious one: that Iran indeed considers it a moral and Islamic duty to help the Palestinian people overcome the historic injustice meted out to them by Israel (and, in this view, the US). This would explain the fact, but not the degree or kind of support, nor why the issue should be labelled as the central issue of Iran's foreign policy.[33] Furthermore there are other Islamic issues that barely get noticed in Tehran, notably Chechnya and Kashmir.[34] Iran admits that its support for the Palestine cause has been the principal problem with third states such as the United States. Moreover Iran's support has been, by its own admission, very costly for Iran.

Why then persist? A strategic argument is sometimes made that if the issue of Israel comes to a conclusion that leaves Israel intact, then this will be the stepping stone to further incursions into the Islamic world by the US and its clients. Or alternatively that, once the Palestine issue is solved, the US will turn to confront Iran. This would account for the role of spoiler that Iran has adopted — for, by insisting on its own principles, it has rejected the idea of interim agreements (Wye, Camp David 2, Sharm el Shaykh, etc.) and partial solutions, even if agreed by the parties concerned. It is Iran's opposition to the peace process more than anything else that accounts for Israeli (and US) opposition to Iran, and not any overriding strategic determination to confront Iran. Iran's policy as motivated by strategic concerns therefore seems circular as an argument and not the prime cause for policy. Nevertheless, it is possible that Iranian leaders consider their role in this region as a potential bargaining card *vis-à-vis* the US in any future negotiations (i.e., Iran seeks a leverage/spoiler role that it can trade at some time in the future for something closer to its direct interests, such as its status as a leading power in the Persian Gulf). Another explanation close to this is the Khamene'i proposition quoted above (and reminiscent of the former USSR), that Iran *has to be consulted* for any issue of international importance to be settled.

Another explanation stems from Iran's regional ambitions. As a Shi'i state Iran has a limited constituency in the Muslim world (Shi'is account for some 15% of all Muslims). Upholding the

Palestinian cause serves as a card for entering regional politics and upstaging the Arab states in the process. Defining it as a 'Muslim issue' gives Iran more leverage, and the country's pretensions to a leadership role are enhanced by activism on this issue. Nor is it reticent about reminding the Arab states of their failure in supporting their brethren: this, contrasted with Iran's selfless efforts, has been a continuing theme in Iranian commentaries.

Focusing on the Palestine issue also has other benefits for Iran. It enables Tehran to emphasise what Iran has in common with the Arab states and to concentrate on their mutual concerns, rather than the issues which do – or might – divide them. Hence, Iran can try and justify its various arms programmes with reference to the alleged threat from Israel, an argument that is accepted in some quarters of the Arab world. Also the territorial dispute with the United Arab Emirates can be put into perspective (i.e. minimised) against the larger threat from Israel.

Iran certainly has an interest in preventing an Iranian–Arab schism developing. Its virtual isolation regionally in the war with Iraq was traumatic. Iran's assumption of an activist role in promoting Palestine as the priority issue serves to diminish this possibility. A related consideration is whether Iran has an interest in stabilisation of the area. Turmoil certainly gives Iran leverage it would not have if the region were quiet. Instability might see the emergence of governments that are radical in ways that some of the Iranian leadership would welcome: hostile to the West and militant in their foreign policies. An unstable region, in this view, plays to Iran's strengths. (This is a view more likely to be entertained by the hard-liners in Iran than by Khatami's reformists.) Certainly, in a vicious circle, Iran's leverage is maximised when things are going badly in the peace process; for that is when Israel and the US are most likely to want Iranian restraint (or assistance), and when Iran will have the least interest in giving it. Conversely, when there is progress, Iran's leverage is reduced, and so also is interest in an Iran that is becoming marginalised.

Palestine policy can be attributed also to Iran's continuing need to demonstrate and affirm and have its principles and the legitimacy of its revolutionary values validated. Keeping the revolution 'awake and vigilant' serves the leadership's domestic needs and priorities, not least in the absence of any discernible domestic strategies. From this perspective, Palestine is a metaphor for the 'epic' of the oppression of Muslims, and Iran's policy an expression of a 'resisting and defiant' nation.[35]

Domestic Politics and the Middle East Question

Support for the Arab cause and the Palestinians came naturally to the Islamic Republic, which was anxious to repudiate *in toto* the legacy left by the preceding regime. This was compounded by the presence of left-wing elements in the revolutionary coalition who injected an ideological dimension into the issue. This, together with the religious dimension (support for fellow Muslims, the loss of Jerusalem, etc.) made a pragmatic approach to the issue all but impossible. Amongst the Iranian leadership, opposition to, and dislike of, Israel stemmed from a sense of humiliation and discrimination that made rational debate more difficult. The new policy was thus simply not questioned, and there has never been a great or continuing debate about this, as there has about relations with the US.

Factionalism in Iran preceded Khatami's ascent, and even when Rafsanjani was President and considered a leading pragmatist, at the time of the Madrid Conference (1991), there was little sign of moderation on the issue of Palestine. All vocal elements rejected the very principle of a Jewish state. While Rafsanjani talked of sending an army to support the Palestinians, Ali Akbar Mohtashemipour called for the assassination of those participating in the Madrid Conference.[36] Mohtashemipour is now part of the Khatami's reformist coalition and an advocate of greater democratisation and social justice on the home front, but he is also a leading hardliner on the Arab–Israeli issue, which is not typical of the reformers.[37] (This underscores the fact that 'reformist' as a general label is not useful; personalities matter and alignments will vary, depending on the issues.) For all that, as one Hezbollah leader observed, there has never been a divergence of views among Iranian officials on the unfairness of the peace process or the right of the Palestinians to resist it.[38]

As we have seen, President Khatami has used much the same

fire-and-brimstone rhetoric as his political opponents, calling Israel a regional and global threat. There is not much to distinguish his position from that of the hard-liners. However Khatami, in contrast to the conservatives, has emphasised Iran's hope for a just, honourable and lasting peace,[39] and he has sometimes suggested that Iran would not undermine any agreement arrived at by the parties themselves (he assured Arafat of this at the OIC meeting in Tehran in December 1997). Hence while Iran had certain ideas about what would constitute a 'sustainable peace', it would not seek to impose them on the parties, or to sabotage any agreement reached by them. This was echoed by Khatami's reformist Minister of Culture, Ataollah Mohajerani, who, on a visit to the area, observed that Syria and Lebanon had a perfect right to conclude any peace agreement that was in their interests, and Iran would not second-guess them on the issue.[40]

The intensification of the rivalry in Tehran between hardliners and reformists reached a climax in the last half of 1999. The reformist press increasingly questioned the received wisdom that the conservatives took for granted, and to which they expected unquestioned obedience. As questions were raised about the conduct of the war with Iraq and the infallibility of the leadership, scepticism became infectious. The most significant event was the trial in autumn 1999 of a prominent reformist with impeccable revolutionary credentials, Abdollah Nouri. In his defence Nouri, with dignity and rigorous logic, posed a number of questions about the regime's policy: why was Iran more adamant and extreme about the issue of Palestine than the parties concerned? What national interest was served by such a policy? Did not dialogue with adversaries make more sense than no contacts at all? Implicitly Nouri raised the question of what were national interests, rather than regime, or even factional, interests. He also brought up the related question of whether posturing amounted to a policy.[41] Although Nouri was convicted, some reformers, emboldened by the new spirit of criticism and questioning, moved the subject of Middle East policy more into the open. Ali Hekmat, editor of *Khordad* (a paper that was banned), observed that 'We have not examined the peace issue carefully, and, even if we had done so, we have not advocated it properly'.[42]

Some Iranian officials sought to convey to Joschka Fischer the idea that a solution to the Lebanon problem would lead to a change in atmosphere between Iran and Israel.[43] This did not happen, and Iran has resisted drawing the line at support for the Hezbollah by extending its support to other groupings. There are several explanations for this. It may be that moderates sought unsuccessfully to limit Iran's commitments to Lebanon. It could also be that the leak was deliberate misinformation. What is clear is that for the Iranian leadership the *intifadah* is an opportunity for political exploitation too tempting to be resisted. Activism abroad is still seen by the Supreme Leader as necessary if the revolution is to be sustained, and if Iran is not to slip back into becoming an 'ordinary' state.

What Could Change Policy?

As the reformers focus on Iran's national interests and push back the areas that have been considered hitherto off-limits, they will eventually start a debate about Iran's Middle East policy – a debate that has yet to take place. This debate could come quicker either as a result of continued deterioration in the region or as a result of the prospect of peace, say between Syria and Israel.

An escalation of hostilities between Israel and Syria could raise questions about Iran's policy just as much as a peace agreement. In the 1980s Iran used the connection with Syria to avoid isolation in the Arab world. It is not clear that Iran has the same degree of need today; however, in continuing the claim to have a 'strategic alliance', Iranian leaders have fostered the impression that they would come to the defence of Syria. Khamene'i has said that Iran will resolutely support and defend Syria under any circumstances, and Defence Minister Shamkhani has warned Israel against attacking Syria or Lebanon.[44]

Even allowing for rhetorical enthusiasm, the question arises whether this is indeed Iran's policy and whether its implications have been assessed or debated. It risks entangling Iran in Syria's quarrels. This might arise from an escalation of hostilities in Lebanon, or it could come about because Syria's relations with Turkey deteriorate. In either case it is questionable whether Iran would want to be directly involved militarily. In the closest shave so far – in October 1998, when Turkey massed troops on the Syrian border demanding the expulsion of PKK leader Abdollah Ocalan – Iran (with Egypt) played an important mediating role to defuse the situation.[45] While Iran has little to lose from continuing turmoil, Syria stands to lose much. Eventually it may again consider a peace settlement with Israel, as it did in 1996 and 2000. In that event, Iran would be powerless to stop it and would have to acquiesce, while trying to maintain its special relationship with Syria.

Another factor that might induce change in Iran's policy is if the cost of playing the spoiler dramatically increased. This could come about as a result of domestic needs and priorities that required a shift in Iran's resources; a weakening of oil prices; entanglements elsewhere; and greater defensiveness on the part of the hard-liners due to domestic pressures and failures. This might see a scaling down of Iran's commitments and assistance to the various rejectionist elements. Recently, Iran is reported to have reduced its military presence abroad.[46] This is in keeping with Iran's continued scaling down of such overseas commitments and attempts to rebuild its traditional diplomatic contacts (e.g. the effort to restore ties with Egypt). These will continue.

A more likely cause of a change in Middle East policy is a rise in the cost of the present policy as a result of international pressure and sanctions. This may happen once the campaign against terrorism resulting from the September 2001 attacks on the United States becomes clearer. Paying a high price for a policy that is reflexively negative and irresponsible might make it easier for the more moderate forces in Iran to press for a change.

Finally inducement might bring about change, if Iran could see or find a useful regional role for itself as a constructive element, in which its interests and, more importantly, status were somehow acknowledged. This requires greater international engagement with Iran, something that is made difficult while Iran persists with its present policies.

I have argued that Iran's approach to the Middle East question has hitherto been largely tactical and ideologically motivated. As a domestic debate on this starts, it is likely to be more critical of this policy than has so far been the case. The policy has been articulated around the need to support the Palestinians, fellow Muslims, an aim that has attracted little dissent. But the issue has not been framed in terms of the best way of assisting the parties to come to an agreement, or in terms of how much of its resources Iran should invest in it and where this issue should rank in Iran's order of priorities. Support for the Palestinian cause is a worthy and popular stance, but whether Iran ought to become a party to the dispute is another matter. The extent, nature and limits of support have not been discussed; they need to be and, as political decisions cease to be the exclusive preserve of a narrow elite, they will be. International factors may make such a change easier, or they may entangle Iran in inadvertent conflict.

Conclusion

Iran's national security policy should be placed in context. It is very much a product of revolutionary Iran's expectations and experience over the past two decades. An exultant phase of initial expansion quickly saw the country mired in war, embattled and self-isolated as a result of its reliance on subversion, terrorism and intimidation. In this era Iran began to look to missiles and WMD. This was driven in part by the lack of effective alternative arms on offer, in part by the lessons derived from the experience of the war, and in part from the country's ambition for status. Yet even in this militant phase of the revolution, certain characteristics of Iran's policies were often overlooked, notably its aversion to risk and its conservatism about territorial change.

Iran is unlikely to abandon all reliance on missiles and WMD, if only because of inertia, prudence and lack of alternatives. As long as it sees missiles as weapons for deterrence and defence, it is unlikely to dispense with them, but there is no reason why measures to reduce the anxiety of other states cannot be undertaken. As for nuclear weapons, such programmes as exist are not irreversible and probably not far advanced. Given a changed situation, they might be easier to arrest and roll-back.

The last five years, corresponding to the Khatami era, have seen major changes in Iran's relations with the world: it is more involved in international and regional affairs, and less isolated, distrusted and feared. However, Khatami's capture of the presidency has resulted in only a marginal change in national security policy. This is in part due to the factional rivalry that persists, which allows each grouping to pursue its favoured policies: greater international engagement or continued agitation, respectively. It is also due to the fact that national security issues are indelibly linked with the identity of revolutionary Iran, the long war with Iraq, and Iran's estrangement from the international community. These, together with a reading of history (with Iran as a victim), make for considerable common ground between the factions on broad issues to do with national security, ranging from the sense of grievance and being wronged historically, through to the desire to play an important role regionally and, if possible, globally.

Despite changes in its foreign policies, Iran's ambitions outpace its resources and still do not reflect a decision to act like an 'ordinary' state. Ideology still drives Iran's Middle Eastern policy, trading on its support for the most extreme Palestinian elements as a means of affirming its Muslim revolutionary credentials and ingratiating itself with the Arab states, while simultaneously undermining them by outbidding them in its support for 'Islamic' causes. In this area, as in the residual support for terrorism associated with the liberation of Palestine, Iran's foreign relations are controlled by elements in its government that fear the *domestic* impact of restraint and normalisation. Unable to meet the country's growing economic needs, the hard-liners seek to retain their constituency by keeping it mobilised and focused on foreign threats and conspiracies, the better to divert attention from their inadequate domestic record. Legitimacy gained through such ventures, however, has a self-limiting quality and offers the regime diminishing returns.

The reformists have not radically changed the content of national security policy; they have changed the context in which it is made. Their contribution has lain not so much in the cogency of their arguments as in the pressures for debate and questioning that they represent and embody. No longer the sacred preserve of a self-designated and self-perpetuating elite, discussion of national security policy has aired and opened up issues that were previously off-limits and subject to automatic acceptance and ritualistic assent. The reformists' positive attitude toward international affairs – treating them as an opportunity and challenge, rather than a threat or burden – now broadly informs Iran's foreign policy (with the exception of the key areas of relations with the US and Israel, which remain controlled by the Supreme Leader).

The more open attitude towards international engagement ushered in by the reformists still has to be translated into the practicalities of national security policy, but even in this tightly controlled domain, the winds of change have been felt. This is most evident in regard to terrorism, as we have seen. In Middle East policy, examining the issues in cost/benefit terms and looking at alternative ways of demonstrating support for beleaguered Muslim cousins will go some way toward breaking the monopoly long exercised by ideologues. Similarly, dragging the issue of nuclear weapons out of the realms of secrecy and cabal and injecting it into a public debate and inquiry certainly makes clandestine programmes harder to hide and justify. Iran's quest for missiles, by contrast, is not much debated or contested; it is accepted as self-evidently legal and (in the absence of funds and reliable suppliers for high-performance aircraft) necessary for defence.

It may be that Iran's covert and unacknowledged quest for nuclear weapons is motivated by the desire to acquire status and legitimacy, to compensate for the country's shrinking economic fortunes. If so, it may be harder to stop than if it is based on an estimate of national security needs. I have argued that, despite instability in Iran's neighbourhood, nuclear weapons are not necessary or even useful for most foreseeable contingencies. The level of public discussion on these issues could be raised, and the limits of, and problems associated with, nuclear weapons, could usefully be underlined. Iran's incipient nuclear programme is constrained by its adherence to the NPT, and this, together with the more open and questioning nature of domestic politics in recent years, might make it harder for clandestine multi-year programmes to continue unnoticed. Where missiles are concerned, the issues are clearer: nothing forbids their possession, and there is no reason to suppose that domestic differences will arise over the need for Iran to assure its own security by continuing to acquire them. That said, there is much that Iran could do to reassure its neighbours. It could desist from bragging or threatening and adopt policies and doctrines that are non-offensive; it could separate missiles from the threat of WMD warheads and enter into strategic dialogues with states (notably Israel) that might misconstrue their intended use.

Future Iranian National Security Policy

The starting point must be domestic politics. Opinions still differ over whether Khatami is the unwitting puppet of a regime that is buying time by allowing him to be its front man – indulging him by permitting a few seemingly inconsequential reforms, while holding on to the key institutions of power – or whether he is a genuine, if cautious, reformer, who prefers incremental change without confrontation but is committed to bringing true democracy to Islamic Iran. A case can be made either way. What is not in doubt is that the reforms to date have been significant, that they reflect popular support and that they have been made with the agreement (or acquiescence) of the Supreme Leader. While no one measure is in itself irreversible, the process of inquiry, debate and criticism is. This makes the reform process open-ended, cumulative and potentially self-reinforcing, not dependent on any one person or limited in time. A number of observations can be made about domestic politics that are uncontroversial.

To begin with, political deadlock along the current lines is likely to continue. This makes decisions like economic reforms (which are politically unacceptable to one faction) unlikely, even though they are pressing, even urgent.[1]

Second, underlying forces in society (notably demographic pressures) make the tide of reform a feature of Iranian politics that will swell, build and envelop the political arena, as the next generation takes a greater interest in politics. This younger generation will need to be accommodated: ineluctably, it will demand more participation in politics and decision-making, from which it has been excluded.[2]

Third, Iran will remain focused on domestic issues and self-absorbed by its 'democratic experiment', but not at the expense of foreign affairs. Debate and questioning of their elders' conventional wisdom ('Iran ever the victim, outsiders always responsible') will characterise the new generation, more knowledgeable and less impressed by traditional claims.[3]

All this will mean that the conduct of foreign affairs will be subject to greater scrutiny and argument; more convincing explanations will be required, along with more exact definitions of national, as opposed to factional interest. Crises like that in Afghanistan – in which Iran contents itself with blaming everyone (Pakistan, the Taliban and the US) and fails to play a role commensurate with its interests – stand out as failures of leadership. Similarly, policies that equate solidarity with the Palestinians to supporting only military solutions, at considerable cost to Iran's own interests, will come in for increased criticism and debate.[4] As resources shrink and competition for resources increases, foreign policies that are costly and not self-evidently in Iran's national interest, may thus become domestic issues.

Consider three distinct scenarios for a future Iran:

i. Continued deadlock, ambivalence and incoherence, with incremental change;
ii. A reformist wave that succeeds in establishing a more truly democratic, accountable regime, together with foreign and security policies that are more transparent;
iii. A conservative coup that reverses the liberalising steps that have taken place and clamps down hard, resulting in a return to more confrontational policies, including meddling in other states.

Such scenarios are inevitably simplistic. It is possible to have a domestic clampdown (iii.) but a continuation and consolidation of a moderate foreign policy. Similarly, a reformist government in true possession of power (ii.) may choose not to pursue more moderate foreign and security policies, perhaps as a concession to its defeated foes, or to establish its nationalist credentials. Domestic pressures provide a context for decisions but do not dictate them.

The most likely scenario is an extrapolation of the current one (i.), though with the proviso that the economic situation (unemployment, brain-drain, disillusionment) is daily creating greater problems of control and credibility for the regime. How long such incoherence and conjuring tricks can forestall the day of reckoning, is uncertain. What is clear is that there is little appetite for violence in contemporary Iran, and discontent will likely be manifested by alienation, dropping out and emigration. So it is possible to envisage a continuation of the current, mixed, system for a while yet. This could lead either to a greater interest in foreign affairs as a vicarious source of legitimacy, or to the reverse (greater introversion as a way to cut costs and liabilities), or to more of the same – a limited opening, as sketched in this paper. Since Iran has invested in improving relations with neighbours, and there is little appetite for isolationism in any of the factions, the most likely scenario is the last one.

What Might Change?

What could change Iran's current policy of cautious and incremental engagement?

- A dramatic deterioration in Iran's immediate security environment (an Iraqi nuclear weapons breakout; a more radical and aggressive Pakistan; a direct clash with Israel).
- Sudden access to a considerable quantity of fissile material, making the acquisition of nuclear weapons technically feasible.
- An abrupt rise in the cost of business-as-usual domestically, necessitating a drastic revision of current policies. This could make foreign policy important either as a diversion or as a means of accessing resources (investment, credits, etc.) to tide the regime over.

None of these appear likely at the time of writing, but none can be excluded either. Oil prices are volatile; when they rise they give the regime's hard-liners a cushion, enabling them to dispense with, or stall, reforms or an opening to the world for capital and investment. When prices decline, as in late 2001, Iran's vulnerabilities are starkly exposed, making Khatami-like reforms and safety valves, indispensable.

Crises can be catalysts for change and cannot be discounted. Repeated international crises have demonstrated the volatility of this region. A sudden shock in Saudi Arabia would make Iran's role in the Persian Gulf more important and make it easier for the US to consider adjusting policy accordingly. Greater doubts about Saudi Arabia might make it prudent for the US to invest greater effort into improving relations with Tehran – and there are areas where tacit cooperation could be extended, whether in post-Taliban Afghanistan, the waters of the Gulf, Iraq, or even the Caucasus. A convergence on the Middle East question – in which Iran became more convinced of the benefits of a diplomatic settlement, and the US appeared more even-handed – may not be imminent, but it is not as improbable as earlier. As Iran looks to its national interests, it might find that the reformists' 'democratic model' has more international resonance and mileage than the contending, exhausted and discredited, 'Islamic revolutionary' model.

Implications for the West

An important question is whether a 'reformist Iran's' goals and interests are compatible with those of the West? I have argued that these interests do indeed largely coincide. The stabilisation of the region through the establishment of regional dialogue and cooperation, the flow of oil and investment, respect for different cultures and traditions as well as support for universal human rights – none of these are areas of divergence.

Iran's struggle to reconcile democracy and Islam and to find an identity that incorporates its pre-Islamic past with its current mixed, modernising condition is of historic importance. In the short term, left to itself, Iran is unlikely to change dramatically: its reforms will remain limited and have an ambiguous impact on its national security policies. It is also likely to persist as a sometimes irritating nationalist feature of the Middle Eastern landscape. However, to the extent that reforms do encourage a more open and pluralist system, and increase the transparency of the regime, they should be welcomed and encouraged. The West has an interest in deepening and expanding this reform movement, though without being identified with it, because that would be to the reformists' detriment. Policies of engagement and inclusion that recognise Iran's legitimate interests as well as its determination to be independent are steps in this direction. The West needs to move on these, but remains constrained by the fact that its actions and concessions might be pocketed without reciprocation and used by the hardliners to shore up their claim that it is the US or West that is the *demandeur* in re-establishing relations. Even so, the West should consider taking the first steps to rebuild relations with Iran.

At the least, if gestures are not reciprocated by Tehran, lack of progress will be seen to result from the refusal of hard-liners within Iran, not from a lack of effort or goodwill on the part of the West. If, as argued here, engagement strengthens moderation and beneficially influences perceptions of security, then engagement is in the West's interests and acts as a means to achieve Iranian moderation rather than a reward to be offered after the event.

Policies that acknowledge positive change in Iran – for example the reduction of its support for terrorism, described earlier – would be helpful.[5] In the past US-led policies that sanctioned and embargoed Iran, especially in the arms area, drove it towards Russian- and Chinese-supplied arms (and reliance on missiles). It is time to re-examine these: recognising Iran's reasonable defence needs, some loosening of restrictions might make it easier for Iran to eschew reliance on some of the unconventional means it has resorted to in the past. The guiding light should be the assumption that, as Iran's sense of embattlement is reduced, it will have less incentive to develop (or continue to develop) weapons of mass destruction and it will be more inclined to engage in discussions about its missile programme in the context of regional arms control.

The reformists may not so far have dramatically changed Iran's national security policies, but they have laid down the basis for modest changes, shaken prevailing images and arrested the inertia characterising revolutionary and confrontational policies. In making Iran more transparent, by introducing debate and analysis into areas previously shielded from them, they have shifted the onus onto those advocating certain policies to justify them and have made covert and illegal programmes harder to sustain. In the process, they have surely given the West reason to feel less threatened by an Iran that is more plural and more open.

Appendix

Institutions and Structures

Institutions

The **Assembly of Experts** (*majlis-e khobregan*) has 86 members, elected by popular vote for an eight-year term (the last election was in October 1998). Members are elected on a provincial distribution of seats. This body selects the Supreme Leader from its own ranks in accordance with Article 107 of the 1979 Constitution. In accordance with Article 111, the Assembly can remove the Supreme Leader if he becomes unable to fulfil his duties, or if he loses one or more of the qualifications necessary to perform his office.

The **Majlis** (*majlis-e shura-e eslami*), the Parliament, is elected every four years and is the main body (lower house) of the legislative branch, solely authorised to enact laws. It can block the President's initiatives and impeach his Ministers.

The **Council of Guardians** (*shura-ye neghaban*) has 12 members; the six clerical members are appointed by the Supreme Leader, and the six jurist members are proposed by the Head of the Judiciary and approved by the *Majlis*. This council determines whether the laws passed by the *Majlis* are compatible with the *shari'a*, Islamic law. It can refer legislation back to the *Majlis* for revision, in effect giving the Council a veto right akin to that of an upper house in a parliamentary system. Under Article 98 of the Constitution, the Council can interpret the constitution, and any such interpretation reached by a three-quarters majority assumes the validity of the

Constitution itself. This makes the Council a quasi-Supreme Court. It can refuse electoral candidates the eligibility to run.

The **Expediency Council** (*majma-e tashkhis-e maslahat-e nezam*) was founded by Ayatollah Khomeini in February 1988. Its principal function is to break stalemates between the *Majlis* and the Council of Guardians and advise the Supreme Leader in accordance with Articles 110 and 112 of the Constitution. With the *Majlis* and Guardianship Council at loggerheads in the current era, the Expediency Council (chaired by Rafsanjani) in theory has plenty of scope for influence.

The **Islamic Revolutionary Guard Corps** (IRGC, or *sepah-e pasdaran-e engelab-e eslami*) was created on 5 May 1979 by a decree of Ayatollah Khomeini. Its primary mission is to protect the revolution and its achievements. A military institution parallel to the regular military, and believed to be more politically inclined, its formal focus is largely, but not exclusively, on threats to Iran and its borders that arise from domestic sources. Since 1985 it has had its own air and naval arms, and in 1982 it established a weapons-procurement organisation and logistical infrastructure and its own Ministry. It has taken the lead in defence production, defence industries and procurement. It now controls missile-related defence activities. In practice it is in competition with the more specialised, and professional, regular military, both for funding and for attention. It is a conservative, leader-dominated military institution parallel to the regular military, although its rank and file are not necessarily more conservative than the regulars.

The **Supreme National Security Council** (SNSC, *shura-e amniat-e melli*) is a committee of 12 permanent members that coordinates all governmental activities related to defence, intelligence and foreign policy. The President acts as chairman, and the members are the heads of the executive, legislative and judicial branches, the chief of the combined General Staff of the Armed Forces, commanders of the IRGC and regular military; the ministers of Foreign Affairs, Interior and Intelligence, affected departmental minister(s), two representatives of the *rahbar*, and the Head of the Plan and Budget Organisation.

Sources: I am indebted to Wilfried Buchta, *Who Rules Iran?* (Washington DC: Washington Institute 2000), chapters 4, 6, 7 and *passim*, and to *Who's Who in Iran* (Tehran: Atieh Bahar Consulting, April 2001).

Structures

Iran's Formal Constitutional Power Structure

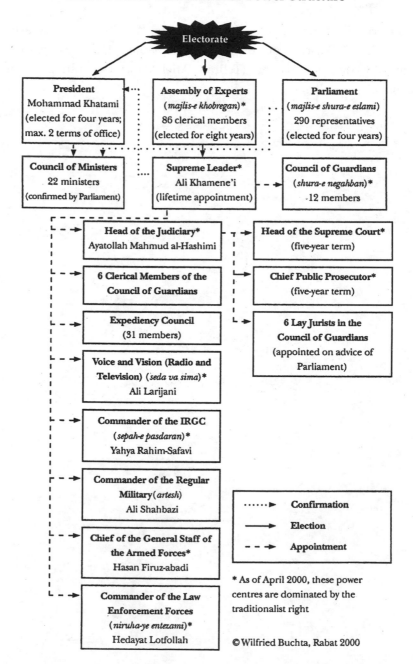

Source Based on Wilfried Buchta, *Who Rules Iran?* (Washington DC: Washington Institute 2000), p. 8. Reproduced with permission.

Iran's Security Organisation

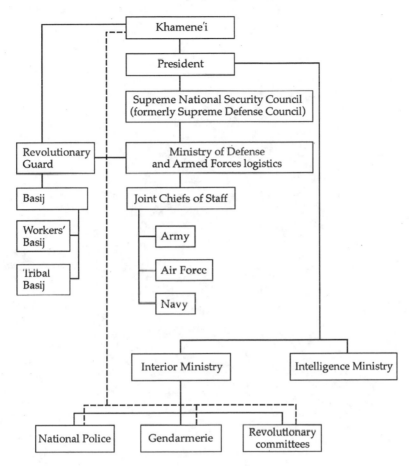

The Supreme Defence Council, which operated during the Iran–Iraq War, subsequently evolved in to the more broadly focused Supreme National Security Council.

Source Shahram Chubin, *Iran's National Security Policy* (Washington DC: Brookings Institution for the Carnegie Endowment, 1994), p. 69.

Notes

Introduction

1 As President Khatami averred in Japan in November 2000; IRNA (Islamic Republic News Agency) in English 1 November 2000, *BBC Summary of World Broadcasts* (hereafter BBC), ME/3987/7–9, 2 November 2000.

Chapter One

1 Mehdi Mozaffari, 'Revolutionary, Thermidorean and Enigmatic Foreign Policy: President Khatami and the "Fear of the Wave"', *International Relations*, August 1999 (vol. XIV, no. 5), pp. 9–28.

2 *Ibid.*, p. 16; 'Roundtable: Iran's Foreign Policy during Khatami's Presidency', *Discourse: An Iranian Quarterly*, summer 2000 (vol. 2, no. 1), pp. 9, 11; and Patrick Clawson, 'Alternative Foreign Policy Views among the Iranian Policy Elite', in Clawson (ed.), *Iran's Strategic Intentions and Capabilities* (Washington DC: Institute for National Strategic Studies, National Defense University, 1994), pp. 27–48.

3 'We are what we are because of our revolutionary thoughts. If we lose this, we shall become something else, we shall become an ordinary country', Rafsanjani Iran TV, 23 August, BBC, ME/2085SI/8, 27 August 1994. This was echoed by *Jomuri-ye Eslami* (editorial), 'Struggling against arrogance is part of the essence of the Islamic revolution and if this is taken away from it, then the revolution will lose its real identity': quoted in Geneive Abdo, 'In Iran, US images as "Great Satan" are Fading', *International Herald Tribune*, 4 November 1999, p. 1.

4 Jalil Roshandel, 'Iran's Foreign and Security Policies: How the Decisionmaking Process Evolved', *Security Dialogue*, March 2000 (vol. 31, no. 1), p. 110.

5 Jahangir Amuzegar, 'Khatami's Economic Record: Small Bandages and Deep Wounds', *Global Dialogue* (special issue *Iran at the Crossroads*), spring/summer 2001 (vol. 3, nos 2–3), pp. 104–14. This author is the foremost analyst of the Iranian economy, and his earlier works, cited therein, give a comprehensive background.

6 Khatami, interview with CNN, Vision of IRI, Network 1, 8 January, in BBC, ME/3120MED/8, 9 January 1998.

7 See especially Wilfried Buchta, *Who Rules Iran?* (Washington DC:

Washington Institute 2000), pp. 11–21.

8 For further details on 'reformist' and 'conservative', see Ali Ansari, *Iran, Islam and Democracy* (London: RIIA, 2000); David Menashri, *Post-Revolutionary Politics in Iran* (London: Frank Cass, 2001) Part 1; Bernard Hourcade, and Nicholas Schwaller, 'La Revolution lente: Iran entre consensus et rupture', in 'Iran: Incertain avenir', *Cahiers de L'Orient* (quatrième trimestre 2000, no. 60), pp. 43–63; and Farhad Khosrokhavar and Olivier Roy, *Comment sortir d'une revolution religieuse* (Paris: Seuil, 1999).

9 Khamene'i, Iran TV, 9 July 2000, BBC, ME/3889MED/14–17, 11 July 2000.

10 See Michael Rubin, *Into the Shadows: Radical Vigilantes in Khatami's Iran*, Policy Paper 56 (Washington DC: Washington Institute for Near East Policy, 2001).

11 Disturbances including the serial killing of intellectuals by the security services in 1998, the student revolt in mid-1999, and further disturbances in 2000 (including political violence by vigilantes) have all been laid at the feet of foreign powers. It is doubtful that Iranians believe a word of it. Cf. Mouna Naim, 'Les Adversaires du Président Iranien sont de plus en plus offensifs', *Le Monde*, 22 July 1999, p. 3; for a recent example see Khamene'i, Voice of IRI, 16 March, Iran radio in BBC, ME/4098MED/8–11, 19 March 2001. As one observer remarked: 'The regime is like a shop that is selling this slogan. ... If they lose this slogan, they have nothing left to sell' (quoted in Elaine Sciolino, 'In Characterizing US, Iran Wants it Both ways', *International Herald Tribune*, 18

March 1999, p. 8).

12 See the hard-line newspaper *Jomuri-ye Eslami*, 10 August, IRNA report in BBC, ME/3303 MED/14, 12 August 1998; Shaul Bakkash, 'Iran's Unlikely President', *New York Review of Books*, November 1998, pp. 47–51.

13 See especially *Norooz* website, Tehran in Persian 22 April in BBC online 24 April 2001; and Morad Saqafi, 'Iran and America: An Unexplained Policy', in *Goftegoo* (Dialogue) spring 2000, pp. 87–101; Roshandel, 'Iran's Foreign and Security Policies', p. 111.

14 Ansari, *Iran, Islam and Democracy*, pp. 129–140.

15 E.g. Minister of Post, Telegraph, and Telephone, Ahmed Mohammedi: 'The more public support a government enjoys, the more it makes other governments behave towards you in a different way', quoted in Molly Moore 'Khatami's New Term Will Test His Resolve', *International Herald Tribune*, 11 June 2001, p. 7.

16 BBC ME 28 February 2000.

17 Khatami TV broadcast 27 May in BBC, ME/3852MED/12–15, 29 May 2000.

18 Mouna Naim, 'La Visite à Paris du president Iranien suscite de vives contestations', *Le Monde*, 25 October 1999, p. 4.

19 Jane Perlez and James Risen 'Clinton Ready to Cooperate, but What About Iran?', *International Herald Tribune*, 4/5 December 1999, p. 3.

20 See especially *Le Monde*, 13 July 1999; Amnon Barzilai and Danile Sobelman, 'Iran's Electoral Revolution Won't Change Policy Regarding Israel', *Ha'aretz*, English Daily Internet Edition, 24 February 2000; and *Yediot Aharonot*, 2 June, in BBC, ME/3858MED/9, 5 June 2000.

[21] See 'Iran's Election' (editorial), *Financial Times*, 12 June 2001, p. 17.

[22] One plausible interpretation of the sentencing of 13 Iranian Jews for 'espionage' was that the hard-liners used their control of the judiciary to sabotage Khatami's foreign policy. Cf. Guy Dinmore, 'Iran's Jews' Appeal Blocked', *Financial Times*, 24 January 2001, p. 9.

[23] See Khamene'i, BBC, 21 April 1998; Voice of IRI, 7 February in BBC Mideast online, 8 February 2001, pp. 30–33; address to Revolutionary Guards 16 January, in BBC, ME/1898MED/10–11, 18 January 1994.

[24] Khamene'i, IRNA, 15 June, in BBC, ME/3562MED/1, 16 June 1999.

[25] Iran TV speech October 8 in BBC, ME/3046MED/13–14, 10 October 1997. 'There is only one nation which has not submitted to this pressure ... We are not prepared to surrender' (Khamene'i, Voice of IRI, 20 April in BBC ME/3822MED/2, 24 April 2000).

[26] 20 April in BBC, *loc. cit.*, 24 April 2000.

[27] Iran TV, 16 November, in BBC, ME/4001MED/9, 16 November 2000.

[28] Iran TV, 12 May, in BBC, ME/2920MED/8–9, 16 May 1997.

[29] Khatami's address to Iranian ambassadors. Iran TV, 13 August 2000 in BBC, MED online, 16 August 2000.

[30] Iran Radio 26 February in BBC, ME/3775MED/10, 28 February 2000.

[31] Khatami, Iran TV July 6 in BBC, ME/3887MED/7–8, July 8, 2000.

[32] Khatami Iran TV 10 February in BBC, ME/4068MED/25–26, 12 February 2001. The President insists that the Islamic Republic is 'meant to serve as role model' and that it is a 'model under

which religion and freedom can live together and alongside each other. And this is a requirement of the age.' See Khatami address to *Majlis* (parliament), Iran TV, 11 March 2001, in BBC, ME/4095MED/esp. 14–18, 15 March 2001.

[33] Khatami, Iran TV, 2 June, in BBC online, 6 June 2001.

[34] Khatami, Iran TV, 11 March, *loc. cit.* in note 32, p. 15.

[35] See Iran radio, 21 August in BBC, ME/3926MED/1–2, 23 August 2000; Stephen Kinzer, 'Strains Showing in Iran', *International Herald Tribune*, 22–23 November 1997, p. 1; Guy Dinmore, 'Iran's President Keeps Nation Guessing Over Re-election Plans', *Financial Times*, 19 February 2001, p. 14.

[36] See Shahram Chubin, 'Iran's Strategic Predicament' *Middle East Journal*, winter 2000 (vol. 54 no. 1), pp. 10–24.

[37] Khosrokhavar and Roy, *Comment sortir ...*, p. 258.

[38] Iran TV, 13 August in BBC online, 16 August 2000, pp. 8–9.

[39] 'Khatami's emergence was thus a response to the call for changes', see Kayhan Barzgar, 'Détente in Khatami's Foreign Policy and its Impact on Improvement in Iran–Saudi relations' *Discourse*, fall 2000 (vol. 2, no. 2), p. 155–78.

[40] Saudi News Agency SPA, Riyadh, 2 June, in BBC, ME/2629MED/3–5, 4 June 1996.

[41] A favourite phrase and implicit condemnation of his predecessors, see Khatami's use of it in his inaugural speech to the *Majlis*.

[42] See Shahram Chubin and Charles Tripp, *Iran—Saudi Arabia Relations and Regional Order*, Adelphi Paper 304 (Oxford: Oxford University Press for IISS, 1996).

[43] Rear Admiral Abbas Mohtaj, IRNA, Tehran, in English, 8 October, in BBC,

ME/3046MED/14, 10 October 1997.

44 IRNA in English, 22 September, in BBC, ME/3648MED/11, 24 September 1999.

45 Khamene'i, Iran TV, 31 October, in BBC, ME/3681MED/7–8, 2 November 1999.

46 See Khatami's comments after his visit to Saudi Arabia, Syria and Qatar, Iran TV, 20 May, in BBC, ME3451MED/7–8, 22 May 1999.

47 Defence Minister Ali Shamkhani, Iran TV, 7 February, in BBC, ME/3760MED/15–16, February 2000. On the offer, see Iran's ambassador to Saudi Arabia, Mohammad Reza Nouri, *Al-Hayat*, London, Arabic, 29 July, in BBC, ME3293MED/1, 31 July 1998.

48 Kamal Kharrazi, the Foreign Minister argued that the principles of foreign policy remain the same but the modes of action could vary. Interview with Al-Jazeera TV, 10 March, in BBC, ME/3787MED/3–8, 13 March 2000.

49 See Roshandel, 'Iran's Foreign and Security Policies,' p. 111; and *Jomhuri-ye Eslami* website, 19 October, in BBC, ME/3977MED/21, 21 October 2000.

50 Iran Radio, 30 April, in BBC ME/2098MED/1–2, 2 May 1997.

51 Text, IRNA news agency, 12 February, in BBC, ME/4070/MED/10, 14 February 2001, on the twelfth anniversary of the *fatwa*. See also, 'Iran and Europe: The Radicals Regret' *The Economist*, 17 October 1998, p. 51.

52 IRNA news agency 4 June, in BBC online, 5 June 2001.

53 The way in which this conference and its proceedings were publicised and depicted, and the severity of the sentences and the attempts to intimidate the reformists in exploiting this event, suggests the degree to which Khatami's foreign contacts and reputation are considered a threat to the conservatives. Similarly, the severity of the sentences appears to have effectively postponed Chancellor Schröder's scheduled visit to Tehran, and to have been designed to do so. See especially 'Iran Silences Dissent', *Financial Times* (editorial), 16 January 2001; Guy Dinmore and Tony Barber 'Dilemmas for EU as Tehran Hardliners Jail Intellectuals' *Financial Times*, 15 January 2001, p. 3; 'Iran: To Prison', *The Economist*, 20 January 2001, p. 40; and 'Bad News for Iran', *International Herald Tribune* (editorial), 18 January 2001, p. 8. Britain's Foreign Secretary, Robin Cook's visit to Tehran in June 2000 was cancelled because of the impending sentencing at that time of 13 Iranian Jews accused of spying; Rosemary Bennett *et al.*, 'Chief Minister's Visit to Iran Cancelled', *Financial Times*, 29 June 2000, p. 10.

54 See Christopher de Bellaigue 'The Struggle for Iran' *New York Review of Books*, 16 December 1999, p. 57.

Chapter Two

1 See the scathing article along these lines applied to Rafsanjani in *Norooz*, Tehran, 14 July, p. 2, in BBC online 31 July 2001.

2 'Today, deterrence no longer comes through armaments alone, in the manner of the Cold War. A cultured manner, along with a thoughtful and considered interaction with others in the world, are more of a deterrent than the presence of vast arsenals', *Hambastegi*, 4 June, p. 3, BBC online, 6 June 2001.

3 Rafsanjani statement in Qom reported in *Asr-e Azadegan* website, 2 December, in BBC,

ME/3709MED/7–8, 4 December 1999.

4 Factionalism and the evolution of political forces also contribute to certain lack of coherence in security policy-making. Cf. Hadi Semati, 'Iran's Priorities', in S. McKnight and N. Partick (eds) *Gulf Security: Opportunities and Challenges for the New Generation*, Whitehall Paper (London: RUSI, 2000), pp. 37–9.

5 For discussions about defence decision-making in Iran, see Shahram Chubin, *Iran's National Security Policy* (Washington DC: Brookings Institution for the Carnegie Endowment, 1994), and Daniel Byman, Shahram Chubin, Anoushirvan Enteshami and Jerold Green, *Iran's Security Policy in the Post-Revolutionary Era* (Santa Monica CA: Rand, 2001).

6 In addition to two terms as President (1989–97), Rafsanjani was formally entrusted with command of the armed forces by Khomeini in the last year of the war with Iraq. It was Rafsanjani who made many authoritative comments about Iran's defence policies and strategy at that time (especially 1987–89). He has continued to do so ever since – and more often than any other civilian – while holding no position related to defence.

7 See Shamkhani statement, BBC 3 August 1998, and *Ha'aretz*, 30 July 1998, quoting an interview in the journal *Iran*.

8 See, for example, Intelligence Minister Ali Yunesi's report to Parliament of his powerlessness in the face of arrests resulting from the conservatives' use of these organs as described: Guy Dinmore, 'Reformists Warn of Hardliners' Threat to Iran's Islamic System', *Financial Times*, 11 April 2001, p. 10.

9 Reportedly 73% of the Guards voted for Khatami. Note also that the regular military have undergone a rehabilitation since the confrontation with the Taliban in 1998. For more detail see Buchta, *Who Rules Iran?* pp. 124–5, 146–8.

10 See respectively Khatami, Iran radio, 21 August, BBC, ME/3296MED/1–2, 23 August 2000; IRNA, 6 December, in BBC, ME/4018MED/10–11, 8 December 2000; and IRNA, 26 November in BBC, ME/4009MED/14–15, 28 November 2000.

11 Khatami, Iran TV, 22 September, in BBC, ME/3032MED/8–9, 24 September 1997.

12 This is Khatami's most extensive commentary on defence issues, covering all aspects of defence; defence expenditures; the right to science and technology; preparedness for deterrence; the threat from Israel; the threat from WMD and the need to ensure their complete and equal elimination, which Iran supports. Speech at the Ministry of Defence, Iran TV, 1 August, in BBC, ME/3296MED/1–4, 4 August 1998.

13 Khatami to *Majlis*, Iran TV, 11 March 2001, in BBC, ME/4095MED/esp. 14–18, 15 March 2001.

14 Eric Arnett (ed.) *Military Capacity and the Risk of War: China, India, Pakistan and Iran* (Oxford: Oxford University Press for SIPRI, 1997).

15 Defence Minister Shamkhani, Vision of IRI Network 1, 7 February 2000, in ME/3760MED/15–16, 10 February 2000.

16 Shamkhani, Vision of IRI Network 1, 6 February 2000, in BBC, ME/4065MED/13–14, 8 February 2001.

17 Indicative of this is the fact that Iranians do not agree on security priorities. See, for example, the

expert panel discussion of this subject in 'New Regional Geopolitical Developments and Iran's National Security', *Discourse*, summer 1999 (vol. 1, no. 1), pp. 5–48.

18 Report by the Presidential Office Centre for Strategic Research and comments by its head, Dr Mohammad Raza Tajik, reported in *Hayat-e Now*, Tehran, 21 August, p. 2, in BBC online 8 September 2001.

19 This is the term used by the Supreme National Council Secretary Hasan Rowhani in a TV interview, 6 February 2000 in BBC, ME3759MED/12–13, 9 February 2000.

20 See Tim Trevan, *Saddam's Secrets* (London: HarperCollins, 1998), pp. 36, 45, 326, 334, and Richard Butler, *The Greatest Threat* (New York: Public Affairs Press, 2000), p. 118, and 'Why Saddam Loves the Bomb', *Middle East Quarterly*, March 2000 (vol. VII, no.1), p. 168.

21 See 'Iraq and Iran Trade Accusations in UN', AP, 20 July 2001, *New York Times* online, 20 July 2001.

22 Reports that Turkey is to get a 'spy satellite' from Israel and to be involved in a regional TMD will increase such concerns. On the former, see 'Satellite Deal Report Upsets Iraq' *International Herald Tribune*, 18 July 2000, p. 10; and Buralk Bekdil and Umit Enginsoy, 'Turkey Sees Shelter in NMD', *Defense News*, 4–10 June 2001, pp. 1, 4.

23 *Tehran Times* (in English) commentary, 8 June, in BBC, ME/3863MED/7, 10 June 2000.

24 Khatami has been among those calling Israel the greatest threat to regional and global peace (*inter alia* on Iran TV, 1 August, in BBC, ME/3296MED/1–2, 4 August 1998). Defence Minister Admiral Ali Shamkhani also identifies

Israel as the greatest threat; see his comments in *Discourse*, summer 1999 (vol. 1, no. 1), pp. 24–25. For a discussion of Iran's perceptions of the US as threat see Saideh Lotfian, 'Threat Perception and Military Planning in Iran' in Eric Arnett (ed.) *Military Capacity and the Risk of War*.

25 *Ma'ariv*, Tel Aviv, 13 August, in BBC, ME/2690MED/18, 14 August 1996.

26 Interview on Iranian TV, 2 August, in BBC, ME/2989MED/6–7, 5 August 1997.

27 Khatami to *Majlis*, Iran TV March 11, 2001, *loc cit.*

28 Voice of IRI, 19 April, in BBC, ME/3206MED/14–16, 21 April 1998.

29 See IRGC Commander, Major-General Mohsen Reza'i, IRNA, 4 May, in BBC, ME/2911MED/11, 6 May 1997; and IRNA in English, 29 June, in BBC, ME/2959 MED/12, 1 July 1997.

30 Reza'i, IRNA in English, 24 September in BBC, ME/2726MED/6–7, 25 September 1996.

31 Khamene'i, Voice of IRI, Network 1, 14 December, in BBC, ME 2796MED/13–14, 16 December 1996.

32 IRNA in English, 18 September 1999, in BBC, ME/3644MED/9–10, 20 September 1999.

33 IRNA in English, 19 September, in BBC ME/3030MED/13–14, 22 September 1997; and IRNA, 21 May in ME/3542MED/6–7, 24 May 1999; and IRNA in English, 1 March in BBC, ME/4085MED/5, 3 March 2001.

Chapter Three

1 Defence Minister Shamkhani,

IRNA in English, 21 August 2001, in BBC online, 22 August 2001.

2   Rafsanjani, interview with *Al Sharq al Awsat* broadcast by MBC TV, in BBC, ME/2803MED/9–12, 24 December 1996.

3   Illegal because there is no international convention or treaty, like the NPT, CWC or BWC, that restricts the transfer of missile or launcher technology, only guidelines agreed by suppliers under the missile technology control regime (MTCR), which do not have the status of a global norm and are not binding on would-be recipients. See also Ali Asghar Keyvani Hosseini, 'The US and the Technological Ban on Iran', *Journal of Defence Policy*, winter 1998/9 (vol. 7, no. 1), pp. 29–68 (in Farsi).

4   Rafsanjani, Friday sermon, Iran Radio, 11 December 1998, in BBC, ME/3049 MED/12–15, 15 December 1998.

5   Khatami, Vision of the IRI, Network 1, 1 August 1998, in BBC, ME3296MED/1–4, 4 August 1998.

6   See Shamkhani statement, Vision of IRI, Network 2, 25 July 1998, in BBC, ME/3289MED/1, 27 July 1998; and *Ha'aretz*, 30 July 1998, quoting an interview in the journal *Iran*.

7   'Iran Plans Military Expansion', *Jane's Intelligence Digest*, 30 November 2000.

8   *The New York Times*, 13 March 2001, ... *News*, 12 March 2001. Rafsanjani ...... to a long-range (250-km) air-... SAM system: see Rafsanjani, IRI, 10 October 1997, in BBC, ME/3048MED/7–9, 13 October 1997.

9   IRNA, quoting from *Kayhan International* (editorial), 29 September 1998, in BBC, ME/3346/MED/8, 1 October 1998; Voice of IRI, external service in English, February in

ME/3454MED/14, 9 February 1999; Vision of Islamic Republic, Network 1, 31 January 2000, in BBC, ME/3753MED/10–11, 2 February 2000; *Arms Control Today*, October 2000, p. 31.

10 Deputy Minister of Post, Telegraph and Telephone, Mehdi Tabeshian, IRNA, 24 June 1999, in BBC, ME/3571MED/8–9, 26 June 1999; for Defence Minister Shamkhani's statements see IRNA in English, 28 December 2000, in BBC, ME/4033MED/7–8, 30 December 2000, and 20 February 2001, in BBC, ME/4077MED/5, 22 February 2001.

11 For this characteristic which is found across the board in contemporary Iranian culture and society, I am indebted to David Menashri of Tel Aviv University. Examples are plentiful: e.g. Iran argues it is a victim of terrorism while practicing it; feels historically aggrieved but rejects its own responsibility when others make similar complaints, etc.

12 President Rafsanjani, interview with *Al Sharq al Awsat*, broadcast by MBC TV, in BBC, ME/2803MED/9–12, 24 December 1996.

13 Shamkhani, Vision of IRI, Network 2, 25 July 1998, in BBC, ME/3289MED/1, 27 July 1998; interview in Iran reported in *Ha'aretz*, 30 July 1998. Other officials emphasised the defence and deterrent function of the missiles; Foreign Ministry spokesman M. Mohamma... noted .... 'solely ... defensive purpo... ...d not for first strike against others' (IRNA in English, 26 July 1998, in BBC, ME/3290MED/1, 28 July 1998); former Guards Commander Mohsen Reza'i also insisted that the missile was for a 'purely defensive purpose and will never be used to initiate an act of

aggression against any country'
(IRNA, 28 July 1998, in BBC,
ME/3292/MED/7, 30 July 1998.
See also Hossein Aryan 'Missile
Development and Iranian
Security', *Jane's Intelligence Review*
September 2001, pp. 38–9.

14 See the Guards Commander,
General Rahim-Safavi, *Kayhan*
website in Persian, 2 July 2000, in
BBC, ME/3885MED/9, 6 July
2000; Safavi also claimed that the
Shihab-3 test was no threat but a
test of defence capability 'within
the framework of deterrence'
Voice of IRI, 15 July 2000, in BBC,
ME/3894MED/11, 17 July 2000.
See also Shamkhani, Vision of the
IRI, Network 1, 23 August 2000,
in BBC, ME/3928MED/12, 25
August 2000, and his comments
that 'Iran follows a deterrent
policy' which requires 'power,
national security and space
technology', IRNA in English, 7
September 2000, in BBC,
ME/3941MED/9, 9 September
2000.

15 Shamkhani, for extensive
comments on missiles in the
context of defence strategy, Vision
of the IRI, Network 2, 30 July
1998, in BBC, ME/3295MED/1–5,
3 August 1998. The Iranian
Ambassador to Saudi Arabia,
Mohammad Reza Nuri, offered to
put the missiles at the 'disposal'
of the Kingdom; see *Al-Hayat* in
Arabic, 29 July 1998, in BBC,
ME/3293/MED/1, 31 July 1998.

16 IRGC Air Force Commander,
Brig.-Gen. Mohammad Baqer
Qalibaf, IRNA in English, 4
August 1998, in BBC,
ME/3298MED/9, 6 August 1998.

17 Khatami at the Ministry of
Defence, Vision of IRI, Network 1,
1 August 1998, BBC, in ME/3296
MED/1–4, 4 August 1998; and at
a UN press conference, 22
September 1998, in BBC, ME/3340
MED/2–3, 24 September 1998.

18 See, respectively, Shamkhani, *Iran
Daily* website in English, in BBC,
ME/3344MED/17, 29 September
1998 and 1 October 1998; and
Foreign Minister Kamal Kharrazi
to Japanese Foreign Minister
Yohei Kono, IRNA in English, 31
October 2000, in BBC,
ME/3986MED/12, 1 November
2000.

19 At a meeting in Qom, *Asr-e
Azazdegan* website, 2 December
1999, in BBC, ME/3709MED/7–8,
4 December 1999. The phrase
echoed the title of an article a
year earlier: 'Israel's Missile
Nightmares', *The Economist*, 26
September 1998, p. 41.

20 Shamkhani quoted in *Al-Ittihad*
(Dubai) and by Gideon Alon in
Ha'aretz, 28 September 1998; and
Hezbollah leader Muhammad
Hussein Fadlallah, Radio Monte
Carlo in Arabic, 1 October 1998,
in BBC, ME/3348/10, 3 October
1998.

21 BBC online, 5 January 2001.

22 For a balanced assessment see
Shai Feldman, 'An Agenda for
Israel's Newly Elected
Government', *Strategic Assessment*,
May 2001 (vol. 4, no. 1), p. 9.

23 Khamene'i, speech in Babol, Voice
of IRI, 17 October 1995, in BBC,
ME/2438MED/12, 19 October
1995.

24 Voice of IRI, 22 September 1998,
in BBC, ME/3340MED/2–3, 24
September 1998.

25 These threats started in early
1990s and persist. See, for
example, Herzl Bodinger, Israeli
Air Force Commander, *Kol Yisrael*,
15 June, in FBIS-NES, 16 June
1992, pp. 16–17; and Gen. Mansur
Sattari, Iran's Air Force
Commander, IRNA, 17 June 1992,
in FBIS-NES, 18 June 1992, p. 40;
for other cases sees Chubin and
Tripp, *Iran—Saudi Relations*,
chapter 3 and footnotes.

[26] Voice of IRI, 22 September 1998, in BBC, ME/3340MED/2–3, 24 September 1998.

[27] Aaron Karp, 'Lessons of Iranian Missile Programs for US NonProliferation Policy', *NonProliferation Review*, spring/summer 1998, pp. 17–26. The author believes that imposing delay on the programme remains feasible but notes the need to engage the country as well. See also US Senate Committee on Governmental Affairs, Subcommittee on International Security, Proliferation and Federal Services Hearing, *Iran's Ballistic Missile and Weapons of Mass Destruction Programs*, 106th Congress, 2nd Session, 21 September 2000 (Washington DC: USGPO, 2000).

[28] Judy Dempsey 'Iran's Missile Capability Worries Israel', *Financial Times*, 12 November 1997, p. 4.

[29] Report on *Jerusalem Post* website, 5 April 2000, in ME/3809MED/11, 7 April 2000.

[30] See *Yediot Aharonot*, 2 June, in BBC, ME/3858MED/9–10, 5 June 2000.

[31] See Sylvain Cypel 'Israel semble annoncer une politique détente envers Teheran', *Le Monde*, 13 July 1999. See also Iranian Foreign Ministry spokesman Hamid Reza Asefi denying a *Ha'aretz* report, IRNA in English, 21 June 1999, in BBC, ME/3568MED/5, 23 June 1999.

[32] Premier Barak's farewell speech to the Knesset appeared to reflect disappointment in this area: 'The sand is running through the timer. Iran is arming itself with missiles and non-conventional weapons', Israel Radio, 7 March 2001, in BBC, ME/4090MED/4–7, 9 March 2001.

[33] The phrase is taken from Mohamed. Kadry Said, 'Missile Proliferation in the Middle East: A Regional Perspective', *Disarmament Forum* (Geneva, UNIDIR), 2, 2001, pp. 49–62. For the growing spread of missiles see also CIA Deputy Director John McLaughlin, 'Watch for More Medium and Long Range Missiles', *International Herald Tribune*, 29 August 2001, p. 6.

[34] *Kayhan International*, 14 August 2001, reported by IRNA in English, 14 August 2001, in BBC online, 15 August 2001.

[35] Khatami, Vision of IRI, 21 September 2000, in BBC, ME/3952MED/7, 22 September 2000.

[36] IRNA in English, 22 March 2001, in BBC, ME/4103 MED/9, 24 March 2001. The missiles were mainly shorter-range battlefield weapons, including *Naze'at*, *Zelzal* and *Fajr*-3. Iran's exhibit was managed by the Aerospace Industries Organization, affiliated with the Ministry of Defence and Armed Forces Logistics, the formal name of the Defence Ministry.

[37] Suggested by Ehud Yaari in email message 16 September 1998.

[38] See for example a commentary on how the US overrates Iran's missile capability and seeks to establish this new 'strategic alliance'. Voice of IRNA, English, 30 August 2001, in BBC online 31 August 2001.

[39] Reformist paper *Aftab-e-Yazd*, BBC online, 24 April 2001. Another paper suggested that ' Today, deterrence no longer comes through armaments alone, in the manner of the Cold War. A cultured manner, along with thoughtful and considered interaction with others in the world, are more of a deterrent than the presence of vast arsenals', *Hambastegi*, 4 June, p. 3, in BBC online 5 June 2001.

[40] Mark Smith 'Verifiable Control of Ballistic Missiles Proliferation', *Trust and Verify*, Jan–Feb 2001, no. 95, pp. 1–3).

Chapter Four

[1] George Perkovich, 'In Tehran, a New Opening to the West is Afoot', *International Herald Tribune*, 3 December 1997, p. 7. For detailed discussion of the status of Iran's nuclear programme and its implications for weapons proliferation see Andrew Koch and Jeanette Wolf, 'Iran's Nuclear Procurement Program: How Close to the Bomb?', *The NonProliferation Review*, fall 1997, pp. 123–35.

[2] Rafsanjani, Voice of IRI, 11 December 1998, in BBC, ME/3409MED/12–15, 14 December 1998.

[3] See respectively IRNA, 17 May 1998, in BBC, ME/3230MED/3–4, 18 May 1998, and Friday sermon, Voice of IRI, 22 May 1988, in BBC, MED/3235MED/2–3, 25 May 1998.

[4] Emphasis added. Khatami, address to the armed forces, Vision of IRI Network 1, 1 August 1998, in BBC, ME/3296MED/1–4, 4 August 1998.

[5] It is worth recalling that Iraq has admitted testing a radiation bomb for planned use against Iran in 1987, see Anthony Cordesman, *Weapons of Mass Destruction in the Middle East* (Washington DC: Center for Strategic and International Studies, July 2001), p. 86.

[6] An Egyptian newspaper's reaction after CIA allegations about Iran's nuclear programme is indicative: 'Considering that Iraq's Gulf adventures have put an end to the entire Arab world's ability to make a nuclear bomb to counter Israel's nuclear arsenal, Iran now seems to be the only solution. It represents a potential regional nuclear counter power to Israeli nuclear threats to the countries of the region.' *Al-Wafd* (Cairo) in Arabic, 7 September 2001, p. 4, in BBC online 9 September 2001.

[7] See Shahram Chubin, 'Does Iran want Nuclear Weapons?', *Survival*, vol. 37, no. 1, spring 1995, pp. 81–104.

[8] Note in this connection *inter alia* the visit by Saudi Defence Minister Prince Sultan to Pakistan's nuclear and missile facilities, which upset the US. Jane Perlez, 'Saudi's Visit to Nuclear Site Alarms US', *International Herald Tribune*, 12 July 1999; see also Richard L. Russell 'A Saudi Nuclear Option?' *Survival*, summer 2001 (vol. 43, no. 2), pp. 68–79. Note the statement of a Kuwaiti military official that, given the small area and the need for defence, thought must be given to 'providing non-conventional deterrents', *Al-Sharq al Awsat*, 2 August 1999, in BBC, ME/3604MED/18, 4 August 1999. For a discussion of some of the issues, see Michael Eisenstadt 'Preparing for a Nuclear Breakout' (2 parts), *Policywatch 550*, Washington Institute for Near East Policy, 8 August 2001.

[9] Cf. Khatami, address to the armed forces, Vision of IRI, Network 1, 1 August 1998, in BBC, ME/3296MED/3, 4 August 1998.

[10] Kamal Kharrazi, then ambassador to the UN, Voice of IRI, Network 1, 23 April 1996, in BBC, ME/2595MED/16, 25 April 1996. A different formulation calls all WMD weapons 'immoral' and therefore impermissible, cf. Shahram Chubin and Charles Tripp, *Iran and Iraq at War* (London: I.B. Tauris/Boulder CO: Westview, 1988), *passim*. (The US

believes that Iran did in fact use chemical weapons against Iraq, although on a smaller scale.)

[11] Notwithstanding attempts to resurrect it. See, for example, IRGC Commander Mohsen Reza'i, extolling the 'culture of martyrdom' as the means to turn Iran into an 'international power', IRNA, 4 May 1997, in BBC, ME/2911MED/11, 6 May 1997.

[12] E.g. the report of the naval exercise *Vehdat*-78 which reported ships taking part in an active air-defence exercise 'during which they, in response to chemical and biological attacks, will defend themselves', Voice of IRI, 27 February in BBC, ME/3776MED/12, 29 February 2000.

[13] See 'Defense Minister Describes Upcoming Victory 8 Exercises', IRNA, 7 October 1997, in FBIS-NES-97-280, 7 October 1997; and 'Iranian Defence Minister Says US Will Use Nuclear Weapons Against Iraq', IRNA in English, 8 February 1998, in BBC, ME/3147MED/16–17, 10 February 1998. Similar loose talk and ignorance was evident in the US war in Afghanistan, when regional 'experts' tortuously argued that US use of nuclear weapons was 'not very unlikely', see *Tehran Times* website in English, 21 October 2001, in BBC online, 22 October 2001.

[14] Cf. Khatami, address to the armed forces, Vision of IRI Network 1, 1 August 1998, in BBC, ME/3296MED/2–3, 4 August 1998.

[15] If this is so, it is worrying indeed, because in the cases of India, Pakistan and South Africa, the officials were 'plugged into' the international strategic community and able to test their concepts and views indirectly and informally against those of the more advanced states. North Korea and others are more problematic, in part because it is impossible to know whether they are aware of others' experiences and of lessons learned, whether about safety, deployment or doctrine.

[16] In the area of decision-making for defence there may be less of this 'horse-trading', but, given the stakes and money involved, a variety of actors must be considered, including the military, the *Pasdaran* (Revolutionary Guards or IRGC), various linked foundations, and others of the inner elite, including those concerned with regime security, such as the intelligence organisations.

[17] 'Iran's Nuclear Programme: Scary or Not?', *The Economist*, 14 March 1998, p. 50; *Salaam* observed: 'It is a sad tale that Iranians should continue to spend money to wait for the day to join the league of nuclear states'.

[18] Mohammad Javad Zarif and Mohammad Reza Alborzi (respectively Deputy Foreign Minister and Director General for International Political Affairs at the Foreign Office), 'Weapons of Mass Destruction in Iran's Security Paradigm: The Case of Chemical Weapons', *Iranian Journal of International Affairs*, winter 1999 (vol. XI, no. 4), pp. 511–53.

[19] These remarks were first reported by the newspaper *Jame'eh*, 27 April 1998; English version found in Farideh Farhi, 'To Have and to Have Not: Iran's Domestic Debate on Nuclear Options', in Geoffrey Kemp (ed.), *Iran's Nuclear Weapons Options: Issues and Analysis* (Washington DC: Nixon Center, January 2001), pp. 35–53, esp. 35–6.

[20] Farhi, *op. cit.* This section leans

heavily on Farhi's article and the citations therein.

[21] Farhi, *op. cit.* (p. 43, note 41), gives the example of *Farda* newspaper.

[22] Farhi, *op. cit.*, p. 48, note 51.

[23] Note however that 'democratic features' might have the unintended effect of making a nuclear programme more subject to public moods and more difficult to renounce. This would argue for quiet diplomacy rather than constant condemnation. On this, see George Perkovich 'Nuclear Proliferation', *Foreign Policy*, fall 1998 (no. 112), p. 21.

[24] E.g. Farhi *op. cit.*, p. 38.

[25] One Iranian analyst has attempted to consider factors that might discourage Iran from weaponising. These include: *inter alia*: improvement of Iran–US bilateral relations; further political liberalisation in Iran; continued improvement of relations with other Middle Eastern states; adoption of doctrines of no-first use of nuclear weapons against non-nuclear weapon states; and denuclearisation of the Middle East: Saideh Lotfian 'Russia's Non-Proliferation Policies: The Case of Iran–Russia nuclear cooperation', *Amu Darya*, winter 2001 (vol. 5, no. 7), pp. 386–7. It is clear that several of these are matters of Iran's own choices: opposition to Israel creates a barrier to regional arms control, as started in the multilateral Arms Control and Regional Security talks started under the auspices of the Madrid Peace Conference of 1991. Similarly, it is worth noting that improved relations with the US would *ipso facto* entail improved relations with Israel, and *vice versa*.

Chapter Five

[1] For example the US Department of State's annual report on terrorism. Two caveats are warranted. Terrorism is a slippery concept, highly context-dependent and politicised, and much contested. Normally it is defined as the indiscriminate use of force for political ends against civilians, intended to inspire fear, horror or psychological reactions beyond the level of violence employed. Second, information on terrorism is inevitably suspect; it is usually controlled and disseminated by government sources, which often have their own agendas as to what is leaked and when. Inevitably, the criticism is made that such information, like the labelling of particular acts, is tainted and selective, depending on the government's political interests.

[2] MENA in Arabic, 1 April 1993, in BBC, ME/1654A/6, 3 April 1993.

[3] Interview by Arye Golan, 26 July 1994, in BBC, ME/2059MED/1, 28 July 1994. Foreign Minister Shimon Peres also noted that all the evidence accumulated after the terrorist attacks against Jewish targets throughout the world pointed to Iran. Voice of Israel, 26 August 1994, in BBC, ME/2085MED/5, 27 August 1994.

[4] Voice of Israel in Hebrew, 3 October 1994, in BBC, ME2118 MED/8, 5 October 1994.

[5] See for example, Jordan's comments after expelling 20 Iranian diplomats: AFP, Paris, in English, 3 February 1994, in BBC, ME/1914MED/9, 5 February 1994; and Yasser Arafat, Palestinian TV, Gaza, in English, 17 March 1996, in BBC, ME/2564MED/11, 17 March 1996.

[6] Rabin, Israel Defence Forces Radio, 6 May 1995, carried by Voice of Palestine, Jericho, in Arabic, 6 May, in BBC ME/2297MED/12–13, 8 May 1995;

Peres, Voice of Israel, Jerusalem, in Hebrew, 21 April 1996, in BBC, ME/2594MED/5, 26 April 1996. Peres also accused Iran of timing bomb attacks to defeat his election bid, ensuring the election of a government less keen on the peace process. See *inter alia* Patrice Claude, 'Shimon Peres accuse l'Iran de vouloir provoquer sa defaite aux elections du mai en Israel', *Le Monde* 18 May 1996, p. 3.

7 For the final communiqué, see Egypt Radio, 23 June 1996, in BBC, ME/2646/MED/2, 24 June 1996.

8 MENA, Cairo, in Arabic 23 October 1993, in BBC, ME/1832MED/11, 29 October 1993.

9 Specific reference is made to Ali Akbar Mohtashemipour, an Iranian official with responsibilities for Lebanon for many years. Voice of Palestine, Jericho, in Arabic, 23 November 1994, in BBC, ME/2162MED/2–3, 25 November 1994.

10 'The ungratefulness of Damascus' (editorial), *Abrar* (International Supplement), 30 December 1995, Tehran in Persian, BBC, ME/25004MED/2–3, 1 January 1996.

11 A report suggested (plausibly) that Rafsanjani himself attributed any Iranian involvement to a decision of the Supreme Leader Khamene'i; See Elsa Walsh, 'Louis Freeh's Last Case', *New Yorker*, 14 May 2001, esp. p. 74. See also the report on the Federal grand jury's findings in mid-2001, which made many references to Iran's involvement but was carefully worded to avoid a direct accusation against Iranian officials or the government in Tehran, which might have led to Congressional pressure for military retaliation.

12 Interview, Iran TV, 2 August 1997, in BBC, ME/2989MED/7, 5 August 1997.

13 'We need to have tolerance, to realize there is a price to pay for everything we want': 'Iran: Reaching Out, If He Can' *The Economist*, 8 August 1998, p. 37.

14 'Mainly' may be more accurate. Iran's hosting of the radical Kurdish PKK appears to be as a form of leverage against Ankara in case Turkey's military co-operation against Iran intensifies. The US State Department suggests that Iran is active in the Gulf, Africa, and Central Asia as well. Nevertheless it is important to note that no major international incident has been attributed to Iran since President Khatami took office in August 1997.

15 IRNA in English, 4 June 2001, in BBC online, 4 June 2001.

16 The State Department's annual report *Patterns of Global Terrorism* (Washington DC: Department of State; Office of the Coordinator for Counter-terrorism, April 2001). This was echoed by the US Assistant Secretary of State Edward Walker, who noted that Iranian support for terrorism had indeed increased.

17 For a discussion of the evolution of Hezbollah tactics, see John Kifner, 'Guerrillas Used Media to Amplify Strikes Against Israel', *International Herald Tribune*, 20 July 2000, p. 2.

18 David Gardner interview with Hezbollah's leader, 'A Modern Shi'ite', *Financial Times*, 8 September 1998, p. 18.

19 Khamene'i, Vision of the IRI, Network 1, 24 April 2001, in BBC online 24 April 2001.

20 Robin Allen, 'Khamene'i Spurns Talks Offer From "Bullying" US', *Financial Times*, 18 October 1999,

p. 5. On the USA's 'impudent' letter, see *Jomhuri-ye Eslami*, 12 September, in BBC, ME/3639MED/9, 14 September 1999.

[21] *Patterns of Global Terrorism 2000* specifically attributes Iran's terrorism to these institutions; for a discussion of them, see Buchta, *Who Rules Iran?*, pp. 156–70.

[22] Note that Mohtashemipour as well as a number of others identified as reformists, such as Abbas Abdi and Said Hajjarian, who had an interest in the Lebanon, assure a certain continuity in policy. (I am indebted to Bill Samii of Radio Free Europe, Prague for this information.) Mohtashemipour organised the conference in support of the second *intifadah* in Tehran in April 2001. Like Mohtashemipour, Hossein Sheikoleslam strongly identifies with the Palestinian cause: 'Palestine — the whole of Palestine — must be liberated', quoted in *Al Hayat*, 30 October 1999, pp. 1, 6, in BBC, ME/3680MED/7, 1 November 1999.

[23] For the background of Iran's relations with the Taleban and the regional context in the immediate period before the September attacks, see Amin Saikal, 'Iran's Turbulent Neighbour: The Challenge of the Taleban', in *Global Dialogue* (special issue *Iran at the Crossroads*), spring/summer 2001 (vol. 3, nos 2–3), pp. 93–103.

[24] Notably Imad Mughniyeh, wanted *inter alia* in connection with major acts of terrorism in the 1980s in Lebanon. Whether it is significant or not, several weeks after the September attacks and the US response Israeli sources reported that Mughniyeh had recently moved from Iran back to Lebanon; see Edward Cody, 'US Takes New Interest in Beirut Terror Suspect', *International Herald Tribune*, 2 November 2001, p. 2.

[25] Making the freezing of their overseas accounts easier. Tom Hamburger, 'US Imposes Sanctions on Hamas and Hezbollah', *Wall Street Journal*, 5 November 2001, p. 3.

[26] Iran unsuccessfully supported a condemnation of US retaliatory strikes against Afghanistan. See James Drummond 'Ministers Seek Diplomatic Balance', *Financial Times*, 11 October 2001, p. 1; and 'Soft Words Uneasy Thoughts', *The Economist*, 13 October 2001, p. 26.

[27] As usual the outcome was a policy of ambiguity. In this case it was evident that the leader was concerned to prevent any steps that might make reconciliation easier. Between the Foreign Minister's meetings with two European delegations he called an emergency SNSC meeting and, exceptionally, chaired it himself. Immediately afterwards he expressed his position noted above to a guaranteed hard-line audience, the families of martyrs of the Iran–Iraq war. Note much of the concern over definitions of terrorism related to US support for Israel. For a concise and incisive report on the politics of Iran's stance see Serge Michel, 'L'Iran est courtisé par les chancelleries occidentales malgré sa position ambigue', *Le Temps* (Geneva), 26 September 2001, p. 5. For the Khamene'i speech, see Voice of IRI, 26 September 2001, in BBC online 27 September 2001. The Iranian position against 'US unilateralism' was amplified at length by Rafsanjani, Voice of IRI, 28 September 2001, in BBC online 29 September 2001.

[28] Speech in Isfahan, Voice of IRI, 30

October 2001, in BBC online 1 November 2001. Khamene'i was aware of the widespread speculation, in the light of comments made by Mohsen Reza'i and subsequent denials and reports, of a trend of signalling and convergence. See Guy Dinmore 'Iran Indicates Support for Anti-Terror Campaign', *Financial Times*, 15 October 2001, p. 1. See also Elaine Sciolino and Neil Lewis, 'Iran Said to Agree to Help US with Rescues', *New York Times*, 16 October 2001; for Iranian denials of secret contacts, see Khatami's comments, 'Iran Denies Secret Contacts with the US', *International Herald Tribune*, 24 October 2001, p. 6.

29 See Guy Dinmore, 'Diplomatic Effort to Engage Iran', *Financial Times*, 24 October 2001, p. 2; and Andrew Parker, 'Foreign Secretary Goes the Extra Mile to Win Over Suspicious Iran', *Financial Times*, 23 November 2001, p. 9.

30 See especially the reports of John Ward Anderson, 'Tehran uses crisis to reinforce its new international influence' *International Herald Tribune*, 8 October 2001, p. 2; Guy Dinmore 'Iran indicates support for anti-terror campaign' *Financial Times*, 15 October 2001, p. 1; and Guy Dinmore, 'Iran fears US may not "finish the job"' *Financial Times*, 16 October 2001, p. 2; 'Saying one thing, meaning another' *The Economist*, 13 October 2001, p. 44.

31 Ayatollah Khamene'i, Voice of IRI, Network 1, 17 October 1995, in BBC, ME/2438MED/12, 19 October 1995.

32 Rafsanjani, Voice of IRI, 20 March 1998, in BBC, ME/3182 MED/8–10, 23 March 1998 Similarly Khamene'i: 'No sir, the Islamic Republic of Iran is not the factor behind Palestine's uprising … .We regard Palestine as a limb of Islam's body. We feel that we are brethren and share the same blood flowing in the veins of the Palestinian youth. But it is they who are driving the Intifadah', Voice of IRI, 20 October 2000, in BBC, ME/3978MED/19, 23 October 2000.

33 Foreign Minister Kamal Kharrazi, support for *intifadah* is central to Iran's foreign policy: IRNA in English, 21 December 2000, in BBC, ME/4031MED/7–8, 23 December 2000.

34 See William Samii, 'Iran and Chechnya: Realpolitik at Work', *Middle East Policy*, summer 2001 (vol. VIII, no.1), pp. 48–57.

35 The language is common to both factions; see especially Khamene'i, who identifies Israel as 'the main problem': 'the feeling of standing up to global arrogance, besides giving national pride and honour to the people for standing up … is also rooted in religion. … The Iranian nation has acted so that there is a power which has stood up to powers such as America's present-day power and machinery', Voice of IRI, 3 November 1999, in BBC, ME3685MED/1–3, 6 November 1999. For Khatami, see especially '[This is] an epic that, on the one hand, demonstrates the injustice … and, on the other, displays a nation's wakefulness and serious determination to attain its most basic rights', Voice of IRI, 25 October 2000, in BBC, ME/3982MED/9, 27 October 2000.

36 For a contemporary report, see 'Iran: Stepping Back into the World', *The Economist*, 16 November 1991, p. 51.

37 At the second international conference in support of Palestine (and the *intifadah*), held in Iran a

decade after Madrid, its Secretary, Mohtashemipour, called for 'resisting aggression by the great powers and their illegitimate representative, the Zionist regime'. See IRNA in English, 22 April 2001, in BBC online 22 April 2001.

38 Deputy Secretary General Shaykh Na'im Qasim, *Al-Mustaqbal*, Beirut, in Arabic, 15 July 2000, in BBC, ME/3895MED/8–9, 18 July 2000. Iranian leaders, in the wake of Khatami's election, were careful to stress that Iran's policies were not subject to change, and that foreign enemies would seek to exploit any differences.

39 See for example his message sent to the Palestinian people, IRNA 29 November in BBC ME/3398MED/6, 1 December 1998.

40 Mohajerani, interview with *Al-Ra'y*, Amman, in Arabic, 28 July 1999, in BBC, ME/3600MED/14–16, 30 July 1999. Contrast this with the conservative view which threatened Syria if it concluded a separate peace: 'The ungratefulness of Damascus' (editorial), *Abrar* (International Supplement), 30 December 1995, Tehran in Persian, BBC ME/25004MED/2–3, 1 January 1996.

41 For a discussion of this episode, see especially Menashri, *Post Revolutionary Politics*, chapter 8, esp. pp. 291–7; Ansari, *Iran, Islam and Democracy*, pp. 196–207. See also 'Abdollah Nouri: A New Pattern for Reformers' in *Iran Farda* (weekly) in November 1999, no. 62, 5/6; for press reports of the trial see esp. 'Saying the Unsayable in Public', *The Economist*, 20 November 1999, p. 58; John Burns 'Iranian Defendant Turns Prosecutor',

International Herald Tribune, 11 November 1999, pp. 1, 4; Geneive Abdo, 'Court in Iran finds Reformer Guilty', *International Herald Tribune*, 13–14 November 1999, p. 1; and Mouna Naim, 'Un ancien ministre condamné à cinq ans de prison', *Le Monde*, 28–29 November 1999, p. 5.

42 Quoted in Guy Dinmore 'Middle East Peace Process Opens up Iranian Ideological Fault Line', *Financial Times*, 21 December 1999, p. 4.

43 *Yediot Aharonot*, Tel Aviv, 16 March 2000, in BBC, ME/3792MED/8, 18 March 2000.

44 Khamene'i, Vision of IRI, Network 1, 23 November 2000, in BBC, ME/4007 MED/7–8, 25 November 2000; and Shamkhani, *Al-Mustaqbal* web site, Beirut, in Arabic, 30 December 2000, in BBC, ME/4034MED/11–12, 3 January 2001.

45 See Ofra Bengio and Gencer Oczan, *Arab Perceptions of Turkey's Alignment with Israel*, BESA Center for Strategic Studies, Mideast Security and Policy Studies, no. 48 (Ramat Gan: Bar-Ilan University, April 2001), pp. 77–81.

46 Some 700 military advisers were recalled from Lebanon, Sudan and Bosnia. See *Financial Times*, 9 November 2001, p. 2, quoting *Frankfurter Allgemeine Zeitung*.

Conclusions

1 See *Global Dialogue* (special issue *Iran at the Crossroads*), spring/summer 2001 (vol. 3, nos 2–3).

2 See notably Geneive Abdo, 'Iran's Generation of Outsiders', *Washington Quarterly*, autumn 2001, pp. 163–71.

3 See Farhad Khosrokhavar and Olivier Roy, Iran: *Comment sortir …*, ch. 5; 'Iran: Incertain

avenir?', *Cahiers de L'Orient*
(quatrième trimestre 2000, no. 60),
esp. pp. 111–29.

[4] Given this record of defining
issues in terms of faction interests,
an Iranian paper recently called
on politicians to clarify what
constitutes national interests: *Iran*

Daily website, Tehran, in English,
12 November 2001, in BBC online,
13 November 2001.

[5] On this, see the sensible
comments by Paul Pillar,
Terrorism and US Foreign Policy
(Washington DC: Brookings
Institution, 2001), pp. 225–6.